THE ROSENBERG COLD WAR SPY TRIAL

A Headline Court Case

Headline Court Cases

THE ROSENBERG COLD WAR SPY TRIAL

A Headline Court Case

Judy Monroe

Enslow Publishers, Inc.

40 Industrial Road	PO Box 38
Box 398	Aldershot
Berkeley Heights, NJ 07922	Hants GU12 6BP
USA	UK

http://www.enslow.com

Library of Congress Cataloging-in-Publication Data

Monroe, Judy.
The Rosenberg Cold War spy trial : a headline court case / Judy Monroe.
    p. cm. — (Headline court cases)
Includes bibliographical references and index.
ISBN 0-7660-1479-7
1. Rosenberg, Julius, 1918–1953—Trials, litigation, etc—Juvenile literature. 2. Rosenberg, Ethel,
1915–1953—Trials, litigation, etc—Juvenile literature. 3. Trials (Espionage)—United States—
Juvenile literature. 4. Spies—United States—Juvenile literature. [1. Rosenberg, Julius, 1918–
1953—Trials, litigation, etc. 2. Rosenberg, Ethel, 1915–1953—Trials, litigation, etc. 3. Spies.
4. Trials (Espionage)] I. Title. II. Series.
KF224.R6 M66 2001
345.73'0231—dc21
        00-011130

Printed in the United States of America

10 9 8 7 6 5 4 3 2 1

To our Readers:
All Internet Addresses in this book were active and appropriate when we went to press.
Any comments or suggestions can be sent by e-mail to Comments@enslow.com or to
the address on the back cover.

Photo Credits: Courtesy of the FBI, pp. 38, 41, 50, 81; Courtesy Harry S Truman
Library, *Dictionary of American Portraits*, Dover Publications, Inc., 1967, p. 22; Courtesy
Library of Congress, *Dictionary of American Portraits*, Dover Publications, Inc., 1967,
pp. 34, 109; Library of Congress, pp. 13, 17; National Archives, pp. 3 (both), 9 (both), 37,
57, 61, 64 (both), 66, 68, 73, 90; United States Holocaust Memorial Museum, p. 20.

Cover Photo: National Archives (both).

Contents

chapter one

ARRESTED AS SPIES

NEW YORK CITY—On Monday evening, July 17, 1950, Julius and Ethel Rosenberg were at home in their small, one-bedroom apartment in New York City. Their two young sons were in the living room. Michael, age seven, was listening to a radio show called "The Lone Ranger," a long-running western adventure program. Three-year-old Robert (Robby, as he was nicknamed) was sleeping.

There was a knock at the apartment door and Julius Rosenberg went to answer it. The man standing at the door said he was an agent with the Federal Bureau of Investigation (FBI). He then told Julius Rosenberg he was under arrest. Ethel Rosenberg began to shout that her husband needed a lawyer. By now, Robby had awakened.

Both sons watched as the FBI agent placed handcuffs on Julius Rosenberg's wrists and led him out of the apartment. Agents then took him into an elevator and put him into a waiting car on the street. From there he was taken to the Federal Court House, Foley Square, New York City, and charged with conspiracy to commit espionage. Conspiracy is a secret plan to commit a crime. Espionage is the act of spying. The FBI claimed Julius Rosenberg was the head of a secret spy ring.

With this charge, the FBI said Julius Rosenberg was a spy for the Soviet Union and had passed secret information about American atomic bomb research to the Soviets during and after World War II (1939–1945). An atomic bomb is an extremely powerful nuclear weapon capable of mass destruction. The FBI claimed the secrets allegedly passed on by Rosenberg helped the Russians build their first atomic bomb in 1949.

While Rosenberg was still at the apartment being arrested, an FBI agent came in and told Ethel Rosenberg and the children to move into the bedroom. They did. More agents streamed in and began to search the small, three-room apartment. They had been instructed to look for papers, books, and jewelry—anything that would show that Julius Rosenberg had extra money to spend as a result of being paid for his spying. That night, Michael listened to the eleven o'clock news on the radio. He heard that his father had been charged with spying, and he would face the death penalty for his crime.

Nearly three weeks later, at about 1:00 P.M., on the afternoon of August 11, two FBI agents stopped Ethel Rosenberg while she was walking to an appointment. Like her husband, she was arrested, charged with conspiracy to commit espionage, and imprisoned. Their sons, Michael and Robby,

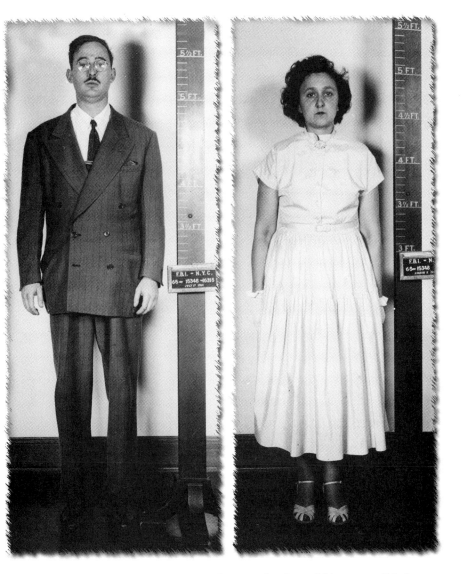

Julius Rosenberg (left) is shown here at the time of his arrest. Ethel Rosenberg (right) had just come from testifying for her husband when she was arrested.

were now without parents, so the boys were placed at first with their grandmother, and eventually, with a foster family. Julius Rosenberg heard about his wife's arrest on a radio news show while he was in jail.

The Rosenberg case would become one of the most talked about espionage cases in the history of American law. Before their arrest, neither Julius Rosenberg nor Ethel Rosenberg had a police record. It was unusual for people without a police record to be charged with such a serious crime. The Rosenberg case lasted for three years, from 1950 to 1953.

chapter two

AMERICA IN THE EARLY 1950s

AMERICA, 1950s—Julius and Ethel Rosenberg were arrested in 1950. At that time, the United States was undergoing major political and economic changes. Fear of spies and atomic bombs was very common. Some of these upheavals and issues of this time would affect the Rosenbergs' case.

End of World War II

World War II (1939–1945) was the world's most costly and devastating war—both in lives lost and in the amount of money spent to wage the war. Millions of people lost their lives. Land and property destruction was widespread. The war grew to include most of the nations of the world. On one side were the Allies—Great Britain, the United States, and the Soviet Union. On the other side were the Axis powers—Germany, Italy, and Japan.

Italy was the first Axis power to surrender in September 1943. Germany surrendered next on May 7, 1945. The Allies now turned their war efforts on Japan.

To force this country to surrender, President Harry Truman of the United States ordered the dropping of the atomic bomb on two Japanese cities: Hiroshima on August 6, and Nagasaki on August 9. One hundred seventy thousand Japanese people died as a result of the bombings.[1] Japan surrendered on August 14, 1945.

The atomic bomb used in Japan was a new type of deadly weapon. Its great explosive force came from the sudden release of nuclear energy. The United States was the first country to test an atomic bomb by exploding one (on July 16, 1945). It was also the first country to use the atomic bomb in a war.

In 1949, the Soviet Union became the second country to develop and test an atomic bomb. Some Americans, including government officials, said that Americans who sympathized with or supported the Soviet Union's Communist views had given that country secrets about how to build the atomic bomb. They based their claim on the belief that the Soviet Union did not have the ability to build the bomb without help.[2]

The Rise of Cold War

Both the United States and the Soviet Union emerged as superpowers after World War II ended. However, the two countries held a deep mistrust of each other. That mistrust first sprang up in November 1917. At that time, the Bolsheviks, or Russian Communists, had seized control of Russia and established the Soviet Union. Communists

A dense cloud of smoke rises more than 60,000 feet into the air over the Japanese city of Nagasaki, the result of an atomic bomb dropped by the United States on August 8, 1945.

supported the idea of common ownership and sharing of labor and products.

After the Bolshevik takeover in Russia, some Americans were affected by the Red Scare. Communists were sometimes called Reds, and widespread distrust of Communists was known as the Red Scare. It was rumored that Communists planned to overthrow the United States government. In fact, some Communists did support extreme measures to retain, restore, or overthrow an existing government. Unease continued to grow between the two countries, but was temporarily on hold during much of World War II. Although both countries fought against Germany during the war, their alliance began to dissolve in 1944.

The Soviet leader at that time, Joseph Stalin, used the Soviet Army to control much of neighboring Eastern Europe as the Nazis retreated. The Soviets were often brutal toward their war enemies and even their own people. President Harry Truman of the United States opposed Stalin's policy of brutality and Communist dominance. He began trying to unite Europe under American leadership. However, as both the United States and the Soviet Union broke various wartime agreements, mistrust grew. Then, in 1946, the United States interpreted a speech by Stalin to mean that communism would take over other governments.

After that, increasing tensions with the Soviet Union resulted in the Cold War. The phrase "Cold War" was popularized by New York journalist Walter Lippmann (1889–1974). He wrote a widely read column for the *New York Herald Tribune* newspaper from 1931 to 1962.

The Cold War was the struggle between the United States and its allies and the Soviet Union and its allies. Direct military conflict did not occur between the two super-powers. Instead, intense struggles erupted continually. During the Cold War, different interests between the United States and the Soviet Union led to mutual suspicion and hostility as both countries tried to promote their political interests throughout the world.

Cold War Escalates

In 1947, to counter the growing Communist presence in Greece and Turkey, President Truman proposed a $400 million aid program for these two countries, to help them resist communism. The next year, the United States launched the $13 billion Marshall Plan to rebuild Western and Central Europe after the great devastation of World War II. Stalin responded by increasing his control over Eastern Europe and threatening Germany's democratic government.

In response to Stalin's actions, in 1949 President Truman helped to create a military alliance called the North Atlantic Treaty Organization (NATO). NATO's original membership included many European countries and the United States. The organization's goal was to guard member countries against takeover by Communists. President Truman also helped to establish an independent West Germany.

The Cold War continued to build. In August 1949, the Communists in China conquered their vast homeland. But when the Chinese Communists signed an alliance with

Stalin, the United States refused to recognize the new government. In Japan, then under American control, economic development was sped up to counter Asian communism.

In a surprise move, Communist North Korea invaded South Korea on June 25, 1950. Chinese Communist forces joined the North Korean Army later in October 1950. To protect South Korea, President Truman sent the American military into action. The Korean War raged until July 27, 1953. By that time, some twenty nations had become involved.

McCarthyism—The Great Red Scare

As the Cold War continued to grow, some Americans developed a profound fear of communism. These people said that the Communists wanted to overthrow the United States government. In addition, they said that the Communists might bomb important American targets to gain control of the United States government.

In early 1950, the United States Congress began a series of well-publicized inquiries into pro-Communist activities by various Americans. Senator Joseph R. McCarthy of Wisconsin (1908–1957) gave his name to this era of intense anticommunist feelings known as McCarthyism. McCarthy was first elected to the United States Senate in 1946.

In 1950, Senator McCarthy claimed that the United States government had employed 205 Communists and he had a list containing the names of those people.[3] He began to accuse various high-ranking officials of subversive

Senator Joseph McCarthy helped fan the fear of communism in the United States during the 1950s.

activities, saying that they were trying to undermine and eventually overthrow the American government. He directly asked people who appeared at congressional hearings if they were Communists or had ever been involved in Communist activities. If they said yes, they were "blacklisted," placed on an official list of people who were disapproved of, punished, or boycotted by the government. They could not find work.

Senator McCarthy continued his investigations during the next three years. In 1953 he became chair of the Senate Subcommittee on Investigations. With his new power, he escalated his investigations against so-called Communists. Many of these investigations focused on finding people who supposedly had given the secrets of nuclear weapons to the Soviet Union during World War II.

These often heated and emotional investigations were widely publicized in national newspapers and magazines. They were often discussed on radio and television shows. Under the pressure of these intense investigations, some former Communists and supposed spies confessed their political activities.

Finally, the public and government officials turned against McCarthy. He was investigated by the Senate, but was cleared of the charges against him. In the end, the Senate censured, or condemned, McCarthy for his abuse of certain senators and Senate committees. His influence on both the Senate and the national political scene began to decrease dramatically. He remained in the Senate until his death on May 2, 1957.

Communism in America

After the Communists seized power in the Soviet Union in 1917, some Americans formed an American branch of the Communist party (CP). The Communist party became a legal political party in the United States. Its numbers continued to grow during the 1930s. By 1939, the American Communist party boasted 100,000 official members and many more followers.[4] By the end of World War II, though, its popularity decreased.

The American Communist party strongly supported equality and social justice. For many party members, communism was simply a philosophy of common ownership and distribution of land and money. It was not a military program to overthrow the existing American democratic government.

During World War II, many American Communists opposed the Axis powers, particularly Germany. Adolf Hitler (1889–1945) was the leader of Germany during World War II. He was also one of the world's most powerful and ruthless dictators, causing the deaths of more than six million Jews and others. One American Communist explained the party's beliefs in the early 1940s, particularly in relationship to World War II: "Being a Communist meant simply to fight for the rights of the people at home, for food and shelter, and to stop Hitler."[5]

Some Americans at that time found anticapitalist philosophies such as communism and socialism appealing. Socialism is a doctrine or movement calling for public ownership of factories and other means of production.

During World War II, many American Communists opposed the actions of Adolf Hitler (shown here reviewing his troops).

Communism, more than any other anticapitalist philosophies, consistently spoke out against religious intolerance and racism, or racial intolerance.

The American Communist party, said sociologist and psychologist Ilene Philipson, "argued louder against racism and anti-Semitism than any other political party in the United States."[6] (Anti-Semitism is discrimination against or intolerance of Jews.) This helps to explain why some Americans, including Jews, embraced the philosophy of communism.

But with the Cold War growing, communism soon became unacceptable. To many Americans, a Communist was a Russian spy or someone disloyal to America and loyal to the Soviet Union.

In late March 1947, President Truman launched a federal loyalty program. This program provided for an extensive background check of all federal government employees. If they were found to be disloyal by being a member of the Communist party or any other organization on the attorney general's "subversive list," federal workers lost their jobs. Once that happened, many could no longer find jobs because they were blacklisted.

Hysteria over communism swept through the federal government and the public. As a result, in 1950, Congress passed the Internal Security Act. This law required the federal registration of all Communist groups and their members. It also made these political beliefs illegal. Now Communists who were not citizens could be deported, or forced out of the United States. They might also be placed in American concentration camps if a national emergency arose, such as another war. During World War II, people of Japanese ancestry had been put in detention camps.

Julius Rosenberg

Both Julius and Ethel Rosenberg were long-standing American Communists. Born on May 12, 1918, Julius Rosenberg was the fourth child of poor Jewish immigrants from Poland. They lived in the part of New York City called the Lower East Side. Immigrants were people who came to live permanently in the United States from another country. Julius Rosenberg's father was a garment worker and his mother stayed home to care for the children.

A rather sickly child, Julius Rosenberg became an avid reader and learner. He focused on studying religion.

Approving of their son's studies, his parents talked about their son someday becoming a rabbi, a spiritual leader among Jewish people. But at age fifteen, Rosenberg discovered an interest that would remain his lifelong passion—politics.

As he was leaving high school one day in 1933, he heard

President Harry Truman started a program in 1947 designed to test the loyalty of employees of the federal government.

a speaker on the street corner near his school. The speaker described how Tom Mooney, a Communist labor leader (someone who represents the interests of workers) on the West Coast, had been unjustly jailed for dynamiting a parade. Rosenberg stopped to listen, donated his allowance of fifty cents to the campaign to free Mooney, and picked up pamphlets on communism, social injustice, and Mooney's cause.

He read all of this material. Soon Rosenberg attended Communist party meetings regularly at a local club and became a member of the Young Communist League (YCL). This organization was for teens and young adults interested in communism. The Young Communist League held occasional dances. Most often at meetings members talked about politics and learned more about communism. Books and pamphlets on communism were readily available and Julius Rosenberg read many of them.

In 1934, at age sixteen, Rosenberg graduated from high school. He enrolled in the School of Technology at the City College of New York (CCNY). The college did not charge tuition. At that time, the school was also a center for political activity.

At college, Rosenberg studied engineering. He also spent a lot of time attending meetings of the Young Communist League that were held regularly on campus. In 1936 he joined the American Student Union (ASU). The union was a newly formed group, made up of members of Communist and Socialist organizations.

To earn money for his subway rides to and from school

and for other expenses, Rosenberg took a part-time job in a drugstore. The store was in a very poor neighborhood. There he saw people even poorer than those in his family's poverty stricken neighborhood.

While at work one evening, a bus ran over an African-American man in the neighborhood. Bleeding heavily, the man was brought into the drugstore. The ambulance took almost an hour to arrive and the man died before the ambulance got there. As Rosenberg cleaned up the dead man's blood, he vowed to never forget his death, which may have been prevented if the ambulance driver had responded sooner. To Rosenberg, the lack of response to this black man's emergency was a "crime."[7] This incident made him more aware of the inequality that existed between the races in the United States, and strengthened his belief in communism.

Along with other Communists, Rosenberg attended many American Student Union and Young Communist League activities: meetings, various fundraisers, and study groups. In December 1936, at age eighteen, he went to a fundraiser for striking seamen, which was held by the International Seamen's Union. (A strike is a work stoppage aimed at getting an employer to better meet the needs of its employees.) Rosenberg came alone. There he met Ethel Greenglass, his future wife.

Ethel Greenglass

Like Julius Rosenberg, Esther Ethel Greenglass grew up amid great poverty on the Lower East Side of New York. She was born on September 28, 1915, and went by her middle name, Ethel. She had a younger half-brother, Sammy, and two younger brothers, David and Bernie. Like her future husband, she was Jewish and a good student. However, she was not encouraged in her studies. Instead of taking pride in Ethel's many accomplishments, her mother constantly belittled and criticized her only daughter. Ethel Greenglass's father, a sewing-machine repairman, worked long hours. He was seldom home.

In spite of her mother's criticisms, Ethel excelled in school. She earned excellent marks and even skipped grades. She also helped at home with her younger brothers. Occasionally, her father took her to the local amateur theaters. In the ninth grade, she acted for the first time, appearing in a school play. From then on, she performed in many school plays and musical productions. Greenglass's ambitions were to become an actress or singer and go to college.

But further education would not be her path. The Great Depression, a severe worldwide economic slump, eventually affected most of the world. It started in the United States on October 29, 1929, when the values of stocks dropped rapidly. Within a few years, much of the rest of the world also suffered from severe economic depression. Millions of Americans lost their jobs in 1930 and 1931.

So, after graduating from high school in 1931, Ethel Greenglass was lucky to find a job. She became a clerk at National New York Packing and Shipping. Because she still lived at home, most of her income went to help her family. She continued to act and sing at productions held in the evenings and on weekends. One day, she found a broken-down, discarded piano. She arranged to have it delivered to her parent's small apartment and taught herself to play.

After that, she went to an audition for the Schola Cantorum. This 250-member citywide chorus sang regularly at Carnegie Hall, a place for professional artists to perform. While at the audition, Greenglass discovered she had a problem; she needed to read music by sight. With her typical determination, she taught herself to sight-read music. When she auditioned several months later, she was accepted as the Schola Cantorum's youngest member. She was only nineteen years old when she joined in 1935.

That same year, Greenglass found a new interest—politics. She had discovered that she was being paid less than others who had been at her company for a shorter time. She joined a labor union, a group of workers who band together to try to improve working conditions. The union went on strike in August 1935, demanding better wages and regular work hours. She supported the strike and joined the strike committee. Soon she was a getting other workers to join the union and the strike.

One night, while Greenglass and other fellow strikers walked home from a meeting, a group of six to ten men rushed at them. The men swung iron pipes at the strikers, seriously hurting some. After beating the defenseless strikers, the men suddenly disappeared. This unprovoked violent act started Greenglass on a quest to find a way to eliminate injustice. Like Julius Rosenberg, that quest led her to embrace communism.

Meanwhile, the strike ended and the workers returned to work. But the members of the strike committee, including Greenglass, were fired. The group appealed their case to the National Labor Relations Board. Although their case took months to wind its way through the system, they won. By this time, however, Greenglass was already working at a new job.

Greenglass continued to sing with the Schola Cantorum, but she stopped after a year. Instead she often sang at political events such as rallies or demonstrations. The Workers' Alliance of America sponsored these events. Formed in March 1935, the Workers' Alliance was made up of socialists and Communists who championed the rights of poor people. In December 1936, Ethel Greenglass accepted a singing job for the International Seaman's Union. Twenty-one-year-old Greenglass came alone, but she left that night with Julius Rosenberg.

Julius and Ethel Rosenberg—The Early Years

The night of the benefit for the International Seaman's Union, Julius Rosenberg noticed Ethel Greenglass from across the room. He walked up to her, introduced himself, and talked a little about himself. Greenglass went on stage and sang. Rosenberg listened, then waited for her as she left the stage. That evening, the two left together.

Rosenberg and Greenglass began spending a lot of time together. They attended many local Communist events such as rallies and meetings. Rosenberg started coming to Greenglass's room at her parents' apartment. While he studied there, Greenglass typed his reports for his college classes. Rosenberg also spent time talking with the younger Greenglass children, especially David. Rosenberg seemed to have influenced David to become a Communist. (David Greenglass joined the Young Communist League when he was a teen.)[8]

After Rosenberg graduated from City College of New York with a degree in electrical engineering, he married Ethel Greenglass on June 18, 1939. Not finding decent jobs in the area, the couple moved to Washington, D.C., in June 1940. There, Ethel Rosenberg took a job as a clerk at the Census Bureau in the United States Department of Commerce. Her job ended when the couple moved back to New York City later that year. Julius Rosenberg had taken a job as a junior engineer for the War Department Army Signal Corps in New York. He inspected electronic equipment.

Julius Rosenberg became an official member of the Communist party on December 12, 1939. He carried a membership card in his wallet. There is no record of Ethel Rosenberg ever being an official member of the party. Both continued to be involved heavily with the American Communist party and its many political events. As required by the party, Julius Rosenberg tried to recruit, or interest, people in joining.

For some time, the Federal Bureau of Investigation (FBI) had been keeping files on many Communists, including the Rosenbergs. As a result, Julius Rosenberg was called to a Signal Corps loyalty hearing in January 1941 and again in March 1941. To keep his job, Julius Rosenberg lied about the couple's affiliation and activities with communism and the American Communist party. The matter was dropped. He went on to get a promotion in October 1942, to Associate Engineer, Inspection. Meanwhile, Ethel Rosenberg took a full-time job with a civilian defense agency.

The young couple had become financially stable. They had a small apartment, one with its own bathroom and kitchen. They even had heat in all the rooms, something Ethel Rosenberg had never had before and Julius Rosenberg had only when he was a teen. Their first child, Michael Allen, was born on March 10, 1943. By then, Julius Rosenberg was traveling a lot for his job, throughout New York, New Jersey, and Pennsylvania.

During the winter of 1943–1944, the couple dropped out of the Communist party and its political activities. As Michael grew into a demanding toddler, Ethel Rosenberg had frequent headaches and often felt dizzy. The couple hired Evelyn Cox to work three days a week at their apartment. She did housework and helped with Michael.

The Rosenbergs Hit Hard Times

Trouble started for the Rosenbergs in 1945. Early that year, the FBI found concrete evidence that Julius Rosenberg was a Communist. It sent two pieces of evidence to the Army Corps: Rosenberg's Communist party membership card that showed he became a member on December 12, 1939, and a copy of a card that showed he had transferred his membership to New York City's Lower East Side Communist Party Club.

When questioned by the Army Corps, Rosenberg lied again. He said he had never been a Communist. This time, however, the Army Corps had firm evidence of his Communist affiliation. He was suspended without pay on February 10, 1945, from his government job. He soon found a job as an assistant engineer with Emerson Radio and Phonograph Corporation, a private company. A little more than a month later, on March 26, 1945, he was officially fired from his government job.

But Rosenberg's luck soon ran out. He lost his job at Emerson on December 7, 1945. He was not let go due to his political activities, though. With the end of World War II, Emerson Radio and Phonograph Corporation lost most of its contracts with the United States Army and Navy. The company was unable to employ so many people and fired many workers, including Julius Rosenberg.

From this time on, a constant lack of money haunted the Rosenbergs. A second child, Robert Harry, was born on May 14, 1947. Meanwhile, Julius Rosenberg could not find work. So he started a small machine shop business with his wife's brothers, Bernie and David. This venture was not successful and eventually ended. Over the next few years, Julius Rosenberg started a handful of similar but unprofitable businesses with Bernie and David. Because these businesses were never very successful, the Rosenbergs had little money.

More and more often, Ethel Rosenberg had to buy food on credit at the neighborhood grocery store. Sometimes she borrowed food from her neighbors and never repaid them.

The Greenglass brothers and Julius Rosenberg often fought over business matters. Finally, their differences proved too great and, in August 1949, Bernie resigned from their latest business venture. Soon after, David also resigned.

Rosenberg was then heavily in debt. He had no business partners and his current business was not doing well. Although the Rosenbergs' money situation had become serious, both remained loving parents to their two young sons.

Michael Rosenberg recalled many fun times while he was young. "My father took me for subway and El [train] rides and played ball with me. We all played cards together. My mother let me type on her typewriter."[9] He remembered that, "they were doting parents" to both of their sons.[10] Both Julius and Ethel Rosenberg shielded their children from the financial problems they were having. But once Julius Rosenberg was arrested on July 17, 1950, the Rosenberg family was torn apart.

chapter three

THE ROAD TO COURT

POLICE WORK—The trail of evidence and events that led to the arrest of Julius and Ethel Rosenberg as Communist spies was full of twists and turns. It was filled with espionage, mysteries, code breaking, and confessions of various accused and confessed spies. The trail is not an easy one to follow. But, it seems to have started in Canada in 1945 and ended in the summer of 1950 with FBI agents knocking at the door of the Rosenbergs' apartment in New York City.

The Beginning of the Trail

Before World War II started, no one knew how to make an atomic bomb. The secrets of atomic fission, the powerful nuclear force behind the atomic bomb, had yet to be discovered. In 1939, President Franklin D. Roosevelt established a small research project on atomic fission. His goal was to beat the Germans at building the world's first atomic bomb. Then the bomb could be used to defeat them during the war.

The project grew to

include research teams at universities around the United States. After a scientist discovered the key to producing atomic fission, President Roosevelt approved the creation of a section of the Army to oversee the building of the atomic bomb. This was called the Manhattan Project. In Los Alamos, New Mexico, a new laboratory was organized to build the bomb. On July 16, 1945, the atomic bomb was successfully tested at Alamogordo, New Mexico. It was dropped, not in Germany, which had already surrendered, but twice in Japan in August 1945, finally bringing World War II to an end.

While the United States was developing the atomic bomb, some high-ranking government officials were concerned that American Communists would leak information about the bomb to the Soviet Union, which at the time was an ally. As a result, the National Security Agency was launched in 1943. Located in Arlington, Virginia, this group was made up of cryptologists (people who study, figure out, and use secret codes), linguists (people who study languages), and mathematicians. The group worked on a code-breaking program called Venona. They began to intercept and break the secret codes of the Soviet Union as World War II continued.

The government's concerns about people sharing information with the Soviets were justified. Leaks about America's atomic bomb program had occurred. The trail that led to the Rosenbergs started with Igor Gouzenko, a Russian code clerk. In 1945, he was in Canada as a member of the Soviet Embassy. About to be called back to the Soviet

Union, he defected (deserted) from Russia and went to Canadian authorities to ask for asylum (to be able to stay in another country). He gave the Canadian government documents from the Soviet Embassy.

Soon after that, Alan Nunn May, a British scientist, confessed to being a spy for the Russians. Information from May and Gouzenko helped lead to the confession of another Soviet spy, Klaus Fuchs, who was living in England.

The Trail Gets Warm

Now, the FBI entered the investigation. The bureau had received information "that the secret of the construction of the atom bomb had been stolen and turned over to a foreign power."[1] A partially burned Russian spy codebook was found on a Finnish battlefield. With this codebook and

May's and Gouzenko's information, the FBI began going through documents that had been stolen from the New York City offices of a Russian spy operation. Eventually the Americans figured out the code for these documents.

In the summer of 1949, one of the decoded documents turned

In 1939, President Franklin D. Roosevelt established a small research project on atomic energy. He wanted to beat the Germans at building the world's first atomic bomb.

out to be a progress report on the Manhattan Project about the creation of the atomic bomb. It was the first time the United States had evidence that spies were working inside Los Alamos, passing information about the atomic bomb to the Russians. The author of the progress report was Dr. Klaus Fuchs. Fuchs was a British scientist at Los Alamos. Had he passed this progress report to the Soviets or had someone else given it to the Soviets?

Both the FBI and the British counterintelligence unit began to investigate Fuchs. Counterintelligence is designed to block an enemy's information sources, to deceive the enemy, and to gather political and military information. Born in Germany, Fuchs had been a member of the German Communist Party in the 1930s. After that, he immigrated to England. As a noted physicist, he was assigned to the British research team that joined the American team at Los Alamos. But Fuchs's name showed up in the documents that Gouzenko had turned over to the authorities and also in documents connected to May.

There was one final piece of evidence that linked Fuchs to the espionage ring. It was another decoded Soviet message that said a British atomic bomb spy had a sister who attended an American college and lived near Boston. Fuchs had a sister who fit both of these requirements during the time of the alleged spying.

Fuchs was then working at an atomic energy research place in England. On December 21, 1949, James Skardon of the British counterintelligence unit talked to Fuchs. Skardon was well known for his ability to hunt and catch spies. His skills worked again. The British arrested Fuchs on February 2, 1950, after he confessed to passing information about the atomic bomb to the Soviets. That next month, he went to trial. He was convicted (found guilty) of espionage and sentenced to fourteen years in prison, the maximum sentence under British law.

The Trail Heats Up

During his confession, Fuchs spoke about a man who called himself Raymond. He would pick up Fuchs's reports and deliver them to the Russians. Although Fuchs did not know Raymond's real name, he gave the FBI a physical description of the man. Raymond had also met Fuchs' sister and her husband. Both gave the FBI a description of Raymond and their descriptions backed up Fuchs' description. The FBI checked their files and came up with three names that could be a match for "Raymond."

After further research, only one name checked out: Harry Gold. Then living in his hometown of Philadelphia, Gold worked as a biochemist. In mid-May 1950, two FBI agents talked to him while he was at work. On May 22, 1950, Gold confessed to being a spy for the Soviet Union for twelve years. Gold had also been the go-between for Fuchs and the Soviets. As further proof, Fuchs identified Gold from photographs the FBI showed him.

Gold confessed to the FBI in great detail. He talked about receiving atomic information and transferring it to his contact in the Soviet Union. He also discussed his life as a messenger for the Soviets. The FBI was able to check out

Dr. Klaus Fuchs (shown here) supplied a steady stream of important American atomic bomb information to Harry Gold, who turned the material over to the Soviets.

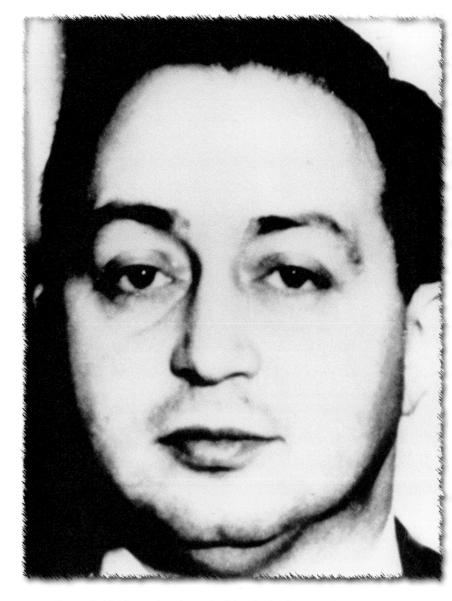

Harry Gold (shown here) testified that he had received spy information from Dr. Klaus Fuchs and David Greenglass.

much of Gold's information, including Gold's Soviet contact who had gone by the name of John.

Under John's instructions, Gold picked up documents from Fuchs and delivered them to John. John also had Gold pick up documents in Albuquerque, New Mexico, from an American soldier who was working on the Manhattan Project in nearby Los Alamos. Gold supplied the FBI with a physical description of this soldier. He also said that the soldier's wife's name was Ruth and that the couple had no children.

Based on Gold's information, the FBI moved even closer to the Rosenbergs. This time, the trail led them to David Greenglass, Ethel Rosenberg's younger brother. David Greenglass had been an Army corporal working as an assistant foreman at the Los Alamos laboratory. During the time he had worked there, the lens mechanism for the atomic bomb was developed. Greenglass's wife's name was Ruth and the couple had no children.

Closing In

To be certain they had the right person, on June 15, 1950, the FBI showed Gold photos of David Greenglass that had been taken in 1945. Gold positively identified Greenglass from the photos. That same day, the FBI talked to David Greenglass who by then lived in New York City.

Like Fuchs and Gold, Greenglass confessed immediately and was charged with conspiracy to commit espionage. He gave the FBI many details about his spying activities for the Soviet Union. He said that he had been a machinist at Los Alamos in 1944–1945 and that he had passed information about the atomic bomb to Gold. After more questioning by the FBI, Greenglass said his wife, Ruth, and brother-in-law, Julius Rosenberg, had also been involved in these activities.

When the FBI questioned Ruth Greenglass, she talked openly. She agreed with the information supplied by her husband about his spying activities. She also said "that her husband looked up to Julius [Rosenberg] with a certain degree of hero worship and that Julius influenced David to think along Communist lines."[2] After many more months of questioning by the FBI, both Greenglasses admitted they had been spies for the Russians under the instructions of Julius Rosenberg and that Rosenberg had headed a spy ring.

Before talking to the Rosenbergs, the FBI conducted more investigations. On July 20, 1950, FBI agents picked up Max Elitcher, a friend and former classmate of Julius Rosenberg's from City College of New York. A Communist, Elitcher was an engineer in the Navy during the war. During questioning by the FBI, he never admitted to any espionage work. He also said he never saw Rosenberg actually involved in spying. However, he claimed that Morton Sobell, a former college classmate and graduate, had been involved with the Rosenbergs in their espionage.

Graduating as an engineer, Sobell worked at the General Electric laboratory in New York City. Elitcher claimed that Sobell had influenced his decision to join the Communist party in 1939. Elitcher also said that Sobell had given the

Born in 1922, David Greenglass was the youngest brother of Ethel Rosenberg. He was a Soviet spy from 1944 to 1946.

Russians important information on military radar systems and radio engineering during the war.

The FBI set out to talk to Sobell, but the engineer, along with his wife and children, had disappeared. Sobell's employer, Reeves Instrument Company, reported that he had not reported to work after June 16, 1950. The FBI tracked Sobell to Mexico City where he was living with his family. After learning that Sobell was wanted by the FBI, Mexican authorities captured him and returned him to the United States. The FBI arrested Sobell on August 18, 1950, in Texas. He was charged with conspiracy to commit espionage.

Julius Rosenberg Is Charged with the Crime

After the FBI arrested Ethel Rosenberg's brother, Julius and Ethel talked about moving away. By then, they both knew they were being watched by the FBI.[3] The press did not report much about what was happening with David Greenglass during June, other than the bare facts about his case. So the Rosenbergs did not know what kind of information Greenglass was supplying to the FBI.

When David Greenglass first mentioned that his brother-in-law had been involved in spying activities during the war, the FBI did not yet know the extent of Julius Rosenberg's involvement. Did he have a minor role or was he an important person in the conspiracy? To find out, J. Edgar Hoover, head of the FBI, wanted his agents to talk to Julius Rosenberg.

Just after 8:00 A.M. on June 16, 1950, FBI agents

knocked on the Rosenbergs' apartment door. Julius Rosenberg let them in. When the agents asked to search the apartment, Rosenberg said no because the agents did not have a search warrant. However, Julius Rosenberg agreed to go with the agents to the Federal Courthouse for questioning. By 3:00 P.M., Rosenberg asked if he was under arrest. When he was told no, he left. He went to talk to a lawyer, Emanuel "Manny" Bloch.

Bloch told Rosenberg not to worry, that his case was routine. Based on Bloch's advice, Julius Rosenberg went home. Meanwhile, the FBI continued to watch Rosenberg. By July 14, David and Ruth Greenglass had begun to supply detailed information to the FBI. Around this time, they named Julius Rosenberg head of a Soviet spy ring during the war.

Based on this latest information, J. Edgar Hoover ordered agents at the New York FBI office to arrest Julius Rosenberg immediately. After getting a search warrant, FBI agents knocked on the door of the Rosenbergs' apartment on July 17, 1950, just before 8:00 P.M. When Julius Rosenberg opened the door, he was handcuffed in front of his sons and wife and taken to the federal courthouse. There he was charged with conspiracy to commit espionage and jailed.

Steps of a Criminal Case

The Rosenbergs' criminal case followed specific legal procedures.

- *Arrest.* After the police or federal government investigates a crime, they file a report describing the crime and naming a suspect. Then they arrest the suspect, or take the suspect into custody.

- *Booking.* At the police station or federal building, the suspect is searched, photographed, fingerprinted, and allowed to contact a lawyer. The suspect is jailed or let go on bail (an amount of money paid in exchange for being let out of jail and agreeing to show up in court).

- *Initial Court Appearance.* At the initial court appearance, the judge informs the suspect of the charge and of the suspect's rights. The judge also decides if the suspect should be released on bail or kept in jail. The suspect's next court date is set.

- *Preliminary Hearing.* A preliminary hearing is called for a suspect accused of a felony. A felony is a serious crime, such as murder or war-time spying. A felony generally is punished by imprisonment or by death. If the judge decides there is enough evidence, the case is forwarded to a grand jury.

- *Grand Jury Indictment.* The grand jury decides if enough evidence exists for the accused to stand trial. If it votes yes, an indictment, a formal charge of a crime, is issued requiring the suspect to stand trial.

- *Arraignment.* The judge reads the charges to the accused. The accused then pleads guilty or not guilty. If not guilty, a date is set for the trial. If guilty, a trial is not held. Instead a date is set for sentencing.

- *Pretrial Hearing.* The judge meets with the attorneys from both sides and reviews the issues of the case.

- *Trial.* The accused, now called the defendant, stands trial before a jury, a group of twelve people who have sworn to decide the facts in a court case and to reach a fair decision. A trial is a formal presentation of the facts of a case by both sides before a jury.

  In a criminal case, the government has the burden of proof. It must persuade the jury that enough facts exist to prove that the defendant is guilty of the crime.

- *Verdict.* After hearing the evidence and testimony in the case, the jury reaches a verdict, or final decision. If not guilty, the defendant is free. If guilty, the defendant is sentenced, or punished.

- *Sentence.* At the end of a criminal trial, the jury or judge decides the punishment.

Rights of the Accused

If someone is arrested and tried on a criminal charge, several amendments to the United States Constitution protect the rights of the accused. These amendments include many safeguards to ensure that procedures are fair. In the Constitution, these safeguards are part of the amendments that make up the Bill of Rights. The Bill of Rights is made up of the first ten amendments to the United States Constitution. It protects the rights of individuals.

- *Fourth Amendment.* Protects against unwarranted search and seizure of property or people. People must give permission or the state must have a search warrant.

  Protects against being arrested without probable

cause. Probable cause exists when the state can demonstrate that the police knew enough at the time of the arrest to believe that an offense had been committed and that the defendant likely committed it. The defendant is the person accused of committing the crime.

- *Fifth Amendment.* Gives the accused the right to remain silent during questioning, protecting against self-incrimination. This means the accused can refuse to answer questions when accused of a crime.

- *Sixth Amendment.* Gives the accused the right to: a lawyer to represent him or her in court; a speedy public trial with a fair or impartial (not biased) jury; be informed of all charges; present witnesses in his or her favor; and cross-examine the government's witnesses. Cross-examination is the questioning of the opposition's witnesses.

- *Eighth Amendment.* Protects against cruel and unusual punishment if convicted and sentenced for a crime.

Pretrial Steps

On the evening of his arrest, Julius Rosenberg was arraigned before United States Judge John McGohey of the Southern District of New York. During an arraignment, the judge reads the charges to the accused. The accused then pleads guilty or not guilty. Manny Bloch was Rosenberg's lawyer.

After pleading not guilty, Rosenberg was returned to jail. He had to wait for a further hearing, this time with a grand jury. The grand jury decides if enough evidence exists for the accused to stand trial. If it votes yes, a court order called an indictment, a formal charge of a crime, is issued requiring the suspect to stand trial.

On August 7, 1950, Julius Rosenberg's case was heard by a federal grand jury. Ethel Rosenberg was called in twice to testify before this grand jury. The first time, on August 8, she testified that she had signed a petition by the Communist party. After that, she did not answer other questions concerning politics. She refused to answer, she said, based on the Fifth Amendment. This amendment grants a person accused of a crime the right to remain silent during court questioning. Ethel Rosenberg could refuse to answer questions that might point to her guilt.

She was requested to appear before the grand jury a second time, on August 11. This time, she was asked nearly identical questions as those from three days earlier. She responded in the same way.

Meanwhile, the grand jury found enough evidence against Julius Rosenberg to require that he stand trial. He was returned to jail. Judge McGohey did not set a court date for the trial.

Ethel Rosenberg is Charged With a Crime

During questioning by the FBI, the Greenglasses had hinted that Ethel Rosenberg may have been involved in spy activities. The FBI launched an investigation of Ethel Rosenberg during the second half of July. Meanwhile, life for Ethel Rosenberg became more difficult.

With the start of the Korean War on June 25, 1950, and

the continuation of the Cold War, Communists and spies were feared and detested by the American public and press. People wondered whether the Korean War might be the start of World War III. Would the United States declare war on the Soviet Union? As the Korean War continued, people began to say that spies like Julius Rosenberg, David and Ruth Greenglass, and Harry Gold should get the death sentence because they were "dangerous traitors."[4]

Ethel Rosenberg's neighbors turned against her. They would not ride on the elevator with her. They would not speak with her. Although she had no business experience, she took over her husband's failing business, in addition to caring for two young sons. By now she was aware of the FBI's investigation of her and she worried about the care of her sons if she, too, was arrested.[5]

After testifying on August 11, 1950, Ethel Rosenberg left the courthouse and began to walk to the subway station. She was on her way to an appointment with the Jewish Community Homemakers Service. She planned to ask this service to place her children in a foster home while her husband was under arrest. Ethel was experiencing various health problems and was trying to balance many things, including the care of her children, at this time. Thanks to two FBI agents who were following her, she never made it to her appointment.

On August 11, 1950, like her husband, Ethel Rosenberg was charged with conspiracy to commit espionage. Before she was jailed, she was allowed to call home. She told her sons, whom she had left with a baby-sitter, that she had been arrested.

On August 17, 1950, a federal grand jury in the Southern District of New York formally charged Julius Rosenberg and Ethel Rosenberg with conspiracy to commit espionage. The Rosenbergs were returned to jail, but in different prisons.

Second Indictment

Based on information from Morton Sobell (who was arrested on August 18, 1950) and other sources, Julius and Ethel Rosenberg were arraigned before United States District Judge T. Hoyt Davis of the Southern District of New York. They were again represented by Manny Bloch. Both pleaded not guilty.

The federal grand jury heard more testimony concerning members of the atomic bomb spy ring. On January 31, 1951, the grand jury issued a second indictment. This one replaced the first indictment. They charged Julius Rosenberg, Ethel Rosenberg, Morton Sobell, and David Greenglass with conspiracy to commit espionage between June 6, 1944, and June 16, 1950. Named as coconspirators, the grand jury said the four had violated a federal law when they had "directly and indirectly, [given] documents, writings, sketches, notes, and information relating to the National Defense of the United States of America" to the Soviet Union during wartime.[6]

On February 2, Julius and Ethel Rosenberg and Morton Sobell pleaded not guilty. The three would be tried at the same time. David Greenglass pleaded guilty. His sentencing

Julius and Ethel Rosenberg (shown here in happier times) were charged with conspiracy to commit espionage.

was postponed until the end of the Rosenberg-Sobell trial, which was set to start on March 6, 1951. It would be held in New York City.

The Judge

Irving R. Kaufman was the judge during the Rosenberg-Sobell trial. Kaufman was known for his stern rulings and his legal brilliance. At age forty, he was also the youngest federal judge.

During a trial, judges should not take sides. The duties of a judge include:

- listening to evidence;
- making certain a defendant's constitutional rights are protected;
- making certain proper legal procedures are followed;
- listening when the lawyers argue over evidence, then deciding, based on rules of evidence, if the evidence should be admitted into the trial.

Jury Selection

Before a trial officially begins, a jury of twelve people is selected by the judge and lawyers for both sides. This process began on March 6, 1951, for the Rosenberg-Sobell trial. All jurors must be impartial, or not biased, against the defendants. The duties of a jury include:

- evaluating the evidence presented at the trial;
- deciding if a defendant is guilty based on whether

the defendant is *guilty beyond a reasonable doubt*; (Reasonable doubt is the highest level of certainty a juror must have to find a defendant guilty of a crime);

- reaching a unanimous decision after hearing all the evidence at the trial;

- announcing a verdict, or decision, to the defendant and judge.

More than three hundred New Yorkers were questioned as potential jurors over one and a half days. From those, eleven men and one woman were chosen. The jurors were mostly accountants and auditors. None of the jurors was Jewish.

Great Pretrial Interest

When the Rosenbergs and Sobell entered the courtroom, the room was packed with reporters and spectators. "Many thought this would be one of the most sensational trials of the century."[7] The media had been watching closely as the spy hunt that had resulted in the arrests of the Rosenbergs, Sobell, and Greenglass unfolded.

The case also held great drama for other reasons. It was hoped that, during the trial, the Rosenbergs would name other members of their spy ring as well as their Russian contacts. During the trial, Americans across the country tuned in to radios and televisions, and read newspapers and magazines so they could learn about the secret atomic bomb spy ring.

The press also speculated about how Ethel Rosenberg

and her brother, David Greenglass, would deal with each other during the trial. The Rosenbergs continued to say they were innocent, while David Greenglass had pleaded guilty. Ethel Rosenberg's family had turned against her and the family feud was of great interest to the public. The feud was widely reported in newspapers and magazines.

Another point of drama was the appearance of United States Attorney Irving H. Saypol, the government's lawyer against the Rosenbergs. The press billed him as a famous hunter of Communists. He had gained his fame by successfully winning federal cases against top American Communists.

Although the courtroom was always crowded, spectators were quiet. Judge Kaufman maintained a serious tone throughout the trial. The Rosenbergs and Sobell were separated and not allowed to speak with each other.

Such high drama, along with the excitement of the trial itself, brought a lot of comments in the press during the trial. This, then, was the emotionally charged setting when the Rosenbergs' trial officially began on the afternoon of Wednesday, March 7, 1951.

chapter four

THE CASE FOR THE FEDERAL GOVERNMENT

NEW YORK CITY—The joint trial of Julius and Ethel Rosenberg and Morton Sobell officially began in New York City on March 7, 1951. The three were charged with conspiracy to commit espionage. The details of their case were recorded on thousands of pages, which resulted in eight volumes or books of records.

The Trial Process

To present the facts in a trial, each side calls witnesses. These are people who come to the witness stand and swear to give truthful testimony or information. Sometimes one or both sides hire expert witnesses. These people have specialized knowledge of a subject and, although they are not part of the case, are allowed to testify in court. Each side can also present evidence. Evidence consists of any physical items or information that might be relevant to the trial. This can include documents, photographs, maps, clothing, and other items.

During a trial, both

sides—the prosecution, in this case the federal government, followed by the defense—present their witnesses and evidence to the jury. During this process, witnesses are called to the witness stand, sworn in (required to tell the truth), and then questioned. Each side calls its own witnesses and questions them on direct examination. They may ask only "direct questions" not open-ended questions that do not suggest a specific answer. For example, "Where were you at 3:00 P.M. on March 15, 1945?" is a direct question.

The prosecuting lawyers present their witnesses and

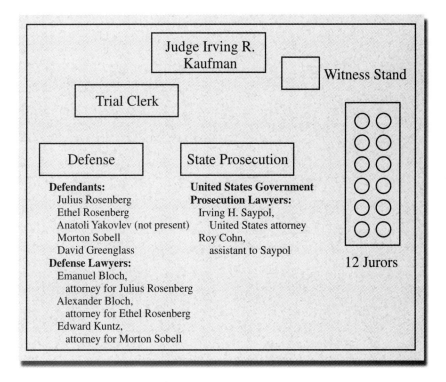

Judge Irving R.
Kaufman

Witness Stand

Trial Clerk

Defense

State Prosecution

Defendants:
Julius Rosenberg
Ethel Rosenberg
Anatoli Yakovlev (not present)
Morton Sobell
David Greenglass
Defense Lawyers:
Emanuel Bloch,
attorney for Julius Rosenberg
Alexander Bloch,
attorney for Ethel Rosenberg
Edward Kuntz,
attorney for Morton Sobell

United States Government
Prosecution Lawyers:
Irving H. Saypol,
United States attorney
Roy Cohn,
assistant to Saypol

12 Jurors

The courtroom as it looked like during the Rosenberg-Sobell trial.

evidence first. The prosecutors try to convince the jury that the defendants are guilty of the charges. The defense then questions the prosecution's witnesses to try to show that the witnesses are not believable, incorrect, or are prejudiced against the defendants. This process is called cross-examination.

Anatoli Yakovlev, David Greenglass, and Morton Sobell

Only the Rosenbergs' and Morton Sobell's case went to trial. Yakovlev, a Russian named as a coconspirator, supposedly had worked with Julius Rosenberg. On the first official day of the trial, March 7, 1951, United States Attorney Irving H. Saypol asked Judge Irving Kaufman to drop Yakovlev from the trial. Yakovlev had left the United States in 1946 and never returned. Judge Kaufman granted this request.

Saypol then asked the judge to drop David Greenglass from the trial because he had already pleaded guilty. Judge Kaufman granted this request, too. The judge would sentence Greenglass at the end of the trial.

The government built its case against Morton Sobell mainly on the testimony of Max Elitcher. Sobell and Elitcher, former fellow students, also had been friends. Elitcher claimed he saw Sobell give a can of microfilm to Julius Rosenberg. In addition to this testimony, Sobell's flight to Mexico and forced return to the United States weighed heavily against him. Sobell's lawyer, Edward Kuntz, could do little to help his client. Sobell was found

In exchange for pleading guilty, David Greenglass was able to keep his wife, Ruth, from being named a coconspirator in the case. She would be able to remain with their two young children.

guilty. Judge Kaufman would sentence him at the end of the trial.

The Prosecution's Strategy

The government's case against the Rosenbergs was based primarily on the testimony of three witnesses:

- David Greenglass, the younger brother of Ethel Rosenberg.

- Ruth Greenglass, wife of David Greenglass.

- Harry Gold, who had already been tried and convicted. He was sentenced to thirty years in jail for being a Soviet spy, based on his conspiracy work with Dr. Klaus Fuchs.

The Prosecution's Opening Statement

On Wednesday, March 7, 1951, the Rosenbergs' trial officially began with an opening statement by the prosecution. Opening statements summarize the strong points of each side's case and what each side intends to prove during the trial. However, nothing the lawyers say during the opening is considered evidence.

In his opening statement, Saypol told the members of the jury it was their duty to protect the rights of all people by moving against anyone who "operated against the Government."[1] He informed them that a grand jury had charged the defendants with conspiracy. He defined conspiracy as "an agreement between two or more people to violate the law—in this case 'espionage on behalf of a foreign power.'"[2]

Saypol then brought up an issue that Bloch objected to, communism. Saypol said that the defendants were not loyal to the United States. Instead, they were loyal to communism in America and throughout the world. Judge Kaufman ruled that matters of communism could be used against the defendants. Throughout the trial, Saypol returned again and again to the issue of the Rosenbergs' helping the Russians at the "expense of disloyalty to the United States."[3]

Continuing with his opening statement, Saypol said that Julius Rosenberg had recruited Morton Sobell and others to get information from various Army, Navy, and national defense plants around the United States. Further, Julius Rosenberg had talked David Greenglass into giving away secrets while he was in the Army at Los Alamos, New Mexico. Greenglass had turned over to Harry Gold stolen atomic bomb sketches and information.

At this point, Manny Bloch requested that a mistrial be declared. In other words, he asked that the trial have no legal effect because of an error or serious misconduct during the proceedings. He said that Saypol's opening statement was inflammatory, that it raised exaggerated emotional responses. He also said that communism was not relevant to this case. The judge refused to declare a mistrial and ordered the trial to continue.

After Saypol's opening statement, the government presented twenty-two witnesses against the defendants. The major damage to the Rosenbergs came from testimony given by David and Ruth Greenglass, Harry Gold, and Max Elitcher. Their testimony gave evidence related to the alleged crime of conspiracy. The government first swore in Max Elitcher.

Max Elitcher

Elitcher's testimony focused on how Julius Rosenberg repeatedly tried to recruit him for espionage. First he explained how he knew Sobell and Rosenberg. Sobell and Elitcher had been high school friends. Later, they both went to the School of Engineering at City College of New York. There, they became friends with Julius Rosenberg. After graduation, Sobell and Elitcher were hired as engineers for the Navy in Washington, D.C., and they rented an apartment together. Elitcher claimed that Sobell introduced him to communism and talked him into joining the Communist party.

In 1944, Elitcher worked on military equipment for the Navy. Specifically, he worked on anti-aircraft control and with systems that controlled the firing of missiles from guns. Around this time, Julius Rosenberg called on him while visiting the Capitol. Rosenberg asked that Elitcher's wife leave the room because he had something private to say. She did.

Rosenberg then asked Elitcher to turn over military equipment information to him for the Russians. He explained that the Soviet Union was being denied war infor- mation. Rosenberg would get the Navy information photographed and returned overnight so there was no risk to

Morton Sobell, a friend of the Rosenbergs, was convicted for his alleged spying activities. After being released from prison in 1969, he wrote an autobiography saying he was innocent.

Elitcher. Rosenberg also mentioned that Sobell was giving military information to him to transfer to the Russians. When Elitcher was undecided about the offer, Rosenberg left his address.

In September 1945, Rosenberg came to Elitcher's home again. The war had already ended. But Rosenberg told him that Russia still needed military information. Meanwhile, Sobell occasionally advised Elitcher to talk to Rosenberg about his work because the Russians could use this information. Late in 1946 or early in 1947, Elitcher telephoned Rosenberg and said he was ready to do espionage work. Rosenberg said no. Why had Rosenberg changed his mind? Elitcher testified, "He felt there was a leak."[4]

Later, during the summer of 1948, Elitcher visited Julius Rosenberg. Elitcher told him that he was leaving his job with the Navy to take a different job. Rosenberg said that was "too bad" because "he [Rosenberg] needed someone to work there for espionage purposes."[5] Sobell was also at this meeting.

A bit later, in July 1948, Elitcher took a ride with Sobell in Sobell's car. Sobell explained that he had a can of camera film that contained valuable espionage information that he needed to get to Rosenberg right away. Sobell put the can in the glove compartment. When he got to his destination, Sobell took the can out and left briefly. When he returned, he no longer had the can and Rosenberg had the information he needed.

During cross-examination, Elitcher testified that Rosenberg had tried to talk him into espionage work at least nine times from 1944 to 1948. Elitcher claimed that he brushed Rosenberg aside each time and never did any espionage work. In 1948, he finally "told Rosenberg that he definitely would not cooperate with him."[6] He said that he never passed any information to Rosenberg or Sobell.

Elitcher never mentioned Ethel Rosenberg. She was apparently never around when Julius Rosenberg had asked Elitcher to spy.

David Greenglass

The next government witness, David Greenglass, took the stand. Under questioning, Greenglass described his work as a machinist for the Army and as an assistant foreman at Los Alamos. He prepared lens molds, usually from sketches supplied by scientists. Those lenses would eventually be used to set off the atomic bomb. Greenglass next described how the Rosenbergs had influenced his decision to become a Communist.

Then David Greenglass launched his first strike against the Rosenbergs. He testified that Julius Rosenberg had known the purpose of the Manhattan Project before Greenglass ever learned what it was. Julius Rosenberg, he claimed, had told David Greenglass's wife the significance of the research there—that Greenglass was actually working on the atomic bomb. Greenglass had only been told that his work was secret. While working at Los Alamos, Greenglass learned the secret identity of various famous scientists working there and gained access to other secret information.

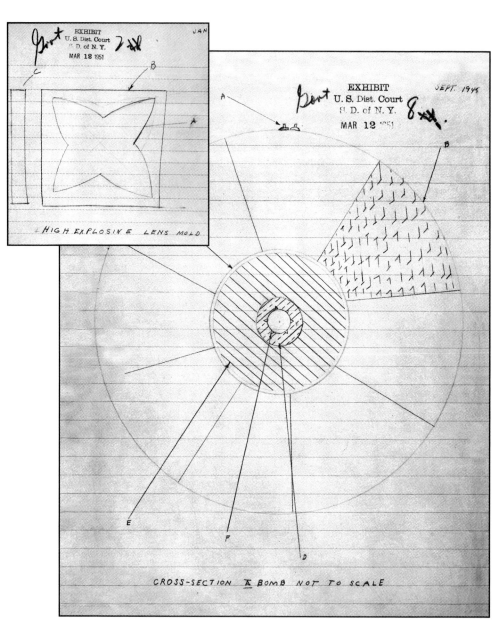

EXHIBIT
U. S. Dist. Court
D. of N. Y.
MAR 12 1951

HIGH EXPLOSIVE LENS MOLD

EXHIBIT
U. S. Dist. Court
S. D. of N. Y.
MAR 12 1951

SEPT. 1945

CROSS-SECTION A BOMB NOT TO SCALE

During the trial, David Greenglass drew a cross-section of the atomic bomb and a sketch of the high explosives lens mold for the atomic bomb. His sketches became part of the trial's evidence.

Recruiting David Greenglass

David Greenglass's second strike against the Rosenbergs came a bit later in his testimony. He said that Ethel Rosenberg had told his wife that Julius Rosenberg was transferring information to the Soviets. He said that both of the Rosenbergs had asked his wife to talk him into being a spy at Los Alamos. At first, Ruth Greenglass refused. Then, she agreed to give her husband the Rosenbergs' request and let him decide what to do.

On November 29, 1944, Ruth Greenglass flew to Los Alamos to visit her husband. At first, David Greenglass said no to being a spy. The next day, though, he changed his mind. His wife then asked him questions about the project, as instructed by Julius Rosenberg. Greenglass supplied her with information on the general layout, the identity of the top scientists there, and the number of people who worked at Los Alamos.

In January 1945, David Greenglass visited his wife in New York City. Julius Rosenberg met with him and asked for "anything of value on the A-Bomb [atomic bomb]."[7] Greenglass agreed to write up his information, along with a list of possible spy recruits. Rosenberg would pick it up the next morning.

Before Julius Rosenberg left, David Greenglass described what an atomic bomb looked like, and explained his work with lens molds. The next morning, Rosenberg picked up Greenglass's written information, sketches of the lens mold, a list of the Los Alamos scientists, and the names of people who might agree to be spies for the Soviets. Julius

Rosenberg told the Greenglasses that Ethel Rosenberg would retype the information.

The Jell-O Box

Soon after this, the Greenglasses went to a dinner party at the Rosenbergs' apartment. There they met Ann Sidorovich of Cleveland, Ohio. Julius Rosenberg said that this woman might visit David Greenglass at Los Alamos to receive atomic bomb information from him. The woman left the apartment and the two couples settled on a plan: Ruth Greenglass would move closer to Los Alamos. When David Greenglass visited his wife, Sidorovich would come to see the couple and pick up atomic bomb information. But what

This is a replica of the Jell-O box that the Rosenbergs and Greenglasses used as a signal of their involvement as spies.

if a different person was assigned to meet with the Greenglasses? How would they recognize him or her?

David Greenglass testified that the four came up with a simple plan using a Jell-O box. Julius Rosenberg tore off a piece of the side of a Jell-O box. The cardboard piece of the box was cut into a pattern. Julius Rosenberg cut a matching piece from the remaining panel. Ruth Greenglass tucked her piece into her purse. Rosenberg kept his piece. The matching pieces would be used for identification purposes. After discussing other arrangements, the Rosenbergs told the Greenglasses not to worry about money. Before leaving, Ethel Rosenberg mentioned she was typing Greenglass's latest handwritten notes.

In the spring of 1945, Ruth Greenglass moved closer to Los Alamos. In early June, a man, later identified as Harry Gold, visited David Greenglass. To verify his identity, Gold told Greenglass, "Julius sent me."[8] Greenglass then took the Jell-O box panel from his wallet. He compared it with the Jell-O box panel Gold had. The two pieces matched. Later that day, David Greenglass gave Gold information on the bomb. He also made sketches of the lens mold and wrote down the names of possible spy recruits. After Gold collected the information and sketches, he left. The Greenglasses then opened an envelope he had given them. Inside was five hundred dollars.

More Espionage

That September, the Greenglasses vacationed in New York City. Julius Rosenberg visited the couple, asking for more bomb information. David Greenglass gave him more, including sketches. Greenglass testified, "I drew up a sketch of the atom bomb and prepared about twelve pages of written material."[9] Both wives were present when this information exchange occurred. Ethel Rosenberg typed Greenglass's information on a portable typewriter.

At this point in his testimony, Greenglass prepared sketches like the ones he had given to Julius Rosenberg. His sketches became evidence in the case. Suddenly, Bloch asked the judge to remove spectators from the courtroom when Greenglass explained the design of the bomb. Why? Bloch said, "to preserve the secret of the atom bomb."[10] Bloch seemed to be saying that David Greenglass was, indeed, a spy, but that the Rosenbergs had not been involved.

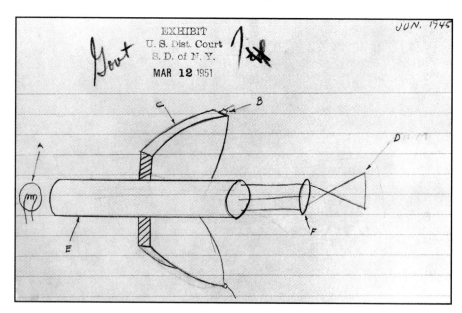

This sketch shows some of the equipment needed for the atomic bomb. This drawing was delivered to Harry Gold.

He was trying to prove the Rosenbergs' patriotism by keeping the sketches secret.

Judge Kaufman agreed to remove the spectators. This may have helped convince the jury that Greenglass "had passed vital secrets to Harry Gold," as instructed by Rosenberg.[11] It also may have helped make Greenglass a credible witness to the jury. It was later learned that the Soviets already had much more accurate information on the atomic bomb than what Greenglass had supplied. That information had come from Dr. Klaus Fuchs.

David Greenglass continued his testimony. He said Julius Rosenberg told the Greenglasses that he had stolen some equipment from his workplace and had given it to the Soviets. After the notes were typed, Julius Rosenberg burned David Greenglass's handwritten notes in a frying pan. He also gave the Greenglasses two hundred dollars.

From 1946 to 1949, while Julius Rosenberg was in business with David and Bernie Greenglass, Rosenberg continued his spy work. Greenglass claimed that Rosenberg had people in New York and Ohio who were giving him information. Rosenberg described how he transferred his information to the Soviets inside a local theater. Rosenberg also told Greenglass that the Russians had given him a watch and a specially made table that was to be used to prepare photos and microfilm.

In February 1950, Julius Rosenberg told David Greenglass to leave America. He explained that a recently arrested spy might talk about other Russian spies. Rosenberg repeated his warning in April. Late in May,

Rosenberg brought the Greenglasses a newspaper that had printed Harry Gold's photo and the story of his arrest. This meant the federal government was closing in on them.

To help prepare for the flight, Rosenberg brought Greenglass a total of five thousand dollars. Rosenberg said the money had come from the Soviets. The Greenglasses had their passport photos taken. Instead of fleeing, David Greenglass testified that he used a little of the money to pay past debts. Most of the rest of the money went to pay his lawyer after his arrest.

David Greenglass's testimony proved very damaging to the Rosenbergs. During cross-examination, Bloch tried to show that Greenglass was not a credible witness and that his information was not consistent. But Bloch's efforts were not successful.

Ruth Greenglass

Ruth Greenglass followed her husband on the witness stand. Although she was never put on trial, she was named as a coconspirator. Most of her testimony covered the same events as that of her husband. Her testimony fully supported what he said. She also added more details about the Rosenbergs' spying activities.

Ruth Greenglass testified that before she visited her husband in New Mexico in November 1944, she talked with the Rosenbergs in their apartment. Julius Rosenberg told her that he and his wife had stopped attending Communist events because "he always wanted to do more than just be a Communist party member."[12] By this, she claimed,

Rosenberg had finally contacted the Russians and "was now doing the work he wanted to do."[13]

At this point, Julius Rosenberg asked Ruth Greenglass to get her husband's help in transferring information from Los Alamos to the Soviets. She said no, but Ethel Rosenberg pressed her to do so. She finally agreed. Julius Rosenberg gave her money to help with travel costs to New Mexico. When she returned to New York City in December 1944, she told Julius Rosenberg that her husband agreed to be a spy. She then told him and also wrote down the spy information David Greenglass had given her. She remembered that Rosenberg was "very pleased."[14]

Julius Rosenberg later helped Ruth Greenglass move to New Mexico to be closer to her husband. Rosenberg told her not to be concerned about money because she would receive money from the Soviets. Soon after that, Ruth Greenglass described the exchange of the pieces of the Jell-O box. Her testimony matched her husband's. Then, in February 1945, just before going to New Mexico, Julius Rosenberg visited Ruth Greenglass in New York City. He gave her instructions about meeting with a contact in New Mexico. That meeting never happened, though, because she became ill.

Ruth Greenglass spoke about another talk she had with Julius Rosenberg. This time, he offered to send the Greenglasses to Russia after Klaus Fuchs and Harry Gold had been arrested. She testified, "he said he was going too," and "would meet us in Mexico" first, before going to the Soviet Union.[15] Ruth Greenglass's testimony, coupled with her husband's, was very damaging to the Rosenbergs.

During cross-examination, Bloch could do little to shake her poise or discredit her information.

Harry Gold

When he took the witness stand, Harry Gold had just begun serving his sentence of thirty years in jail. His sentence had been based on his conspiracy work with Fuchs and the fact that he had received documents from David Greenglass. Gold had been a spy for the Soviets for fifteen years.

Gold first testified that, in late May 1945, Yakovlev had given him instructions about an upcoming spy meeting with David Greenglass. Yakovlev gave Gold a piece of paper with the name Greenglass typed on it, an address in New Mexico, and a secret message to say, "I am from Julius."[16] Yakovlev also gave Gold a piece of cardboard cut from a Jell-O box and told him that Greenglass would have the matching piece. Finally, Yakovlev gave Gold five hundred dollars in an envelope to give to Greenglass. If Greenglass was not in, Gold was to get the spy information from Greenglass's wife.

Gold arrived in New Mexico on June 2, 1945. When he went to the address Yakovlev had given him, the Greenglasses were not in. He rented a room for the night and returned the next day. The prosecution presented a copy of the hotel registration where Gold claimed to have stayed while in New Mexico. Gold's date and hotel name matched the hotel's registration form.

When Gold knocked on the door, David Greenglass opened it. Gold said, "I am from Julius."[17] He held out the piece from the Jell-O box. Greenglass let Gold in, went to a

After chemist Harry Gold confessed to being a Russian spy for twelve years, he was jailed for thirty years.

woman's purse, and took out a piece of cardboard. He compared it with Gold's piece. The two Jell-O box pieces matched. Both pieces were returned to their original places.

David Greenglass passed his atomic bomb information to Gold. Gold gave Greenglass the envelope containing the money. Then David Greenglass gave the Rosenbergs' telephone number to Gold. A few days after returning to New York City, Gold transferred Greenglass's atomic bomb information to Yakovlev.

Much of what Gold covered in his testimony actually related to the Greenglasses and Fuchs, not the Rosenbergs. After Saypol finished examining Gold, the jury was excused until the next morning.

Gold returned the witness stand, ready for cross-examination. But Bloch did not cross-examine him. Gold was excused from the witness stand in less than one minute. It is unusual in a criminal case for the defense not to cross-examine a prosecution witness. Bloch must have feared that Gold would damage the Rosenbergs with other information.[18]

Series of Witnesses

The government called a series of witnesses to testify. None presented a great deal of evidence against the Rosenbergs. Together, though, their testimony helped solidify the government's case against the Rosenbergs.

Dr. George Bernhardt, the Rosenbergs' family doctor, took the witness stand. He said that in May 1950, Julius Rosenberg had asked for information about shots needed to go to Mexico. After Dr. Bernhardt gave him the information, Rosenberg said he needed to know for a friend. This bit of testimony supported David Greenglass's claim that Julius Rosenberg had urged him to go to Mexico.

Ben Schneider, a photographer, said that in May or June of 1950, Julius and Ethel Rosenberg and their two boys had come to his business. He took thirty-six photographs of the whole family. Julius Rosenberg requested that the photos be of passport size. Rosenberg then said he and his family were going to France. Schneider's testimony gave more weight to the idea that the Rosenbergs were preparing to leave the United States.

Evelyn Cox testified that sometime in 1945, she saw a new table in the Rosenbergs' living room. Cox had worked part-time for the Rosenbergs as their housekeeper. She described the table, which was the one supposedly used for work on spy photos. When she asked Ethel Rosenberg where the table came from, Rosenberg said it had been a gift to her husband. Cox's testimony about the table differed from Ruth Greenglass's testimony. Greenglass claimed that Rosenberg said he bought the table at a department store.

The government also produced records from the bank where Ruth Greenglass said she had deposited four hundred of the five hundred dollars given to them by Gold on June 3, 1945. Ruth Greenglass had testified that she had put four hundred dollars into this bank account on that date. Evidence like this helped build the government's case against the Rosenbergs.

Elizabeth Bentley

Elizabeth Bentley was the prosecution's last witness. The media called her the "Red Spy Queen" since she often testified at Communist spy trials. Because she was paid to testify, she was considered an expert witness.

Bentley stated that she had joined the American Communist Party in 1935 and had engaged in spying activities until 1945. That summer, she became an ex-Communist and told the FBI about her spying activities. The FBI asked her to continue her spy work, but this time under its guidance. She accepted the assignment.

She first testified that a Communist spy she worked with, Jacob Golos, had gotten an envelope from a man. She claimed that this man looked like Julius Rosenberg. She gave a general physical description of him. However, she could not identify Rosenberg positively from photos. She explained that she had not gotten close enough to see the man's face clearly. This incident had occurred in 1942. Since the Rosenberg conspiracy had not started at that time, according to the formal charges, this information could not be used as evidence.

Next, she said that she had gotten five or six telephone calls from a man who asked to talk with Golos. Each time, the caller began his conversation with, "This is Julius."[19] These calls were made in the fall of 1942 through November 1945.

Although the jury may have found Bentley's testimony convincing, it actually proved nothing. Spies commonly use false names to protect their true identity. The caller may or may not have been Julius Rosenberg. So after great buildup in the press, Bentley's trial testimony was not particularly useful to the prosecution. Further, Bentley had testified in dozens of other trials—for a fee. The fact that she was paid to testify, and had done so on many other occasions, greatly reduced her credibility.

Prosecution Ends Its Case

After Bentley stepped down from the witness stand, Saypol said that the prosecution had closed its case. This end seemed abrupt. The federal government originally had said it would call more than one hundred witnesses, but instead presented many fewer.

The defense asked the judge to dismiss the case, but Judge Kaufman denied the request. Now it was the defense's turn to call their witnesses to the stand.

chapter five

THE CASE FOR JULIUS AND ETHEL ROSENBERG

NEW YORK—The federal government had presented quite a bit of strong and damaging evidence against the Rosenbergs, mainly through the testimony of David Greenglass, Ruth Greenglass, and Harry Gold. The defense had a difficult job ahead, to try to counter this evidence. The two main defense witnesses were Julius Rosenberg and Ethel Rosenberg. Both denied any involvement in any spying activities. Throughout the trial, they continued to declare their innocence.

The Defense's Strategy

The defense lawyers were:

- For Julius Rosenberg—Manny Bloch

- For Ethel Rosenberg—Alexander Bloch

- For Morton Sobell—Edward Kuntz

The defense tried to prove that the Rosenbergs were not guilty of their crimes. Proof consisted of having the Rosenbergs deny and counter each of the specific charges that government witnesses had made against them. The defense did not call any friendly witnesses. This meant that they had no witnesses testify on behalf of the Rosenbergs.

Based on the advice of lawyer Edward Kuntz, Morton Sobell did not testify. Kuntz advised this strategy because Sobell claimed that he had not been involved in the Rosenberg conspiracy to commit espionage.

The Defense's Opening Statement

The quiet courtroom was packed with reporters and spectators when Manny Bloch gave his opening statement for Julius Rosenberg. He told the jury that the defendant had been arrested in July 1950 and since then had continued to proclaim his innocence. He reminded the jury to stay unbiased, not to be prejudiced. But he admitted that Julius Rosenberg had been charged with a serious crime.

Next, he said that the federal government would not be able to prove its charges against Rosenberg beyond a reasonable doubt. Then he asked the members of the jury "to keep [their] minds open" and to "be fair."[1] He repeated this plea several more times during his opening statement. He went on to stress that they, the members of the jury, needed to decide a verdict based on the evidence alone, not on politics. He finished by again asking jurors to keep open minds.

Alexander Bloch, Manny Bloch's father, stood up next. His opening statement for Ethel Rosenberg was brief.

He asked the jury not to find her guilty simply because her brother had confessed to being a spy. He told the jury that she was a housewife and had no involvement in a spy ring. By naming Ethel, her brother and sister-in-law would get better treatment. And, in fact, Ethel Rosenberg's brother got a light sentence and his wife was never tried.

Bloch finished by asking the jury to keep an open mind until all the testimony had been presented. The jury, he said, would then find that Ethel Rosenberg was crime-free. She "should be sent back to her family to take care of her children," he concluded.[2]

Defense's First Witness—Julius Rosenberg

The defense called its first witness, Julius Rosenberg. After eight months in prison, Rosenberg had had time to think about how to speak on his own behalf. He had decided which questions he would answer and which ones he would refuse to answer. Manny Bloch agreed with Rosenberg's strategy. However, Alexander Bloch disagreed with some of Rosenberg's strategy.

After Julius Rosenberg was sworn in, Manny Bloch asked him a series of questions about his marriage. Rosenberg also described his three-room apartment, how much he paid in rent, and other expenses during his marriage. All these basic living expenses could be paid with what Rosenberg was earning as a government employee. The couple, according to Rosenberg, did not have extra money to spend on costly clothing, furniture, or parties. This testimony went against what the Greenglasses had said— that the Rosenbergs were spending large sums of money on entertainment.

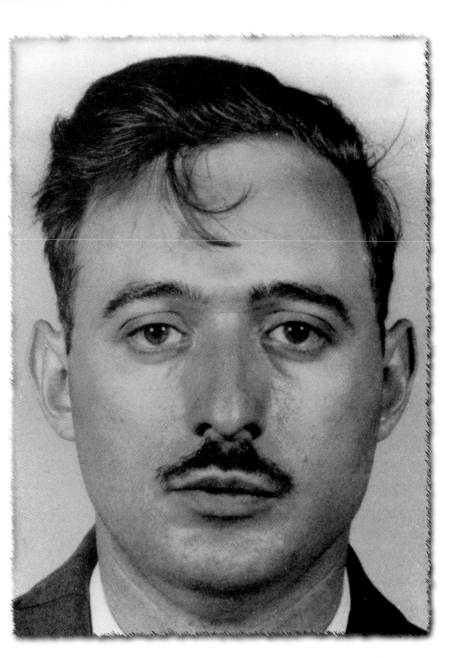

Julius Rosenberg testified on his own behalf during the trial.

Julius Rosenberg's Political Views

Judge Kaufman asked Rosenberg questions about his political beliefs. Rosenberg started out by saying that he thought the justice systems in both the United States and the Soviet Union had favorable points. He "approved" of the American system and said, "I owe my allegiance [loyalty] to my country at all times."[3] Bloch then took over the questioning and asked Rosenberg if he owed loyalty to any other country. Rosenberg said no and was willing to fight for the United States in times of war.

Julius Rosenberg then began to explain the Soviet Union's accomplishments under communism. According to Rosenberg, Russia had worked hard against illiteracy [the inability to read], carried out a lot of construction, and helped defeat Adolf Hitler during World War II. Because America was so anticommunist in 1951, his speech was brave. Rosenberg was speaking openly about his political views, specifically communism, but his openness soon passed. Judge Kaufman asked if he had been a member of any group that talked about Russia's government. Rosenberg hedged, not answering directly. Finally he said, "I feel at this time that I refuse to answer a question that might tend to incriminate me."[4]

Rosenberg had used his Fifth Amendment right against self-incrimination. According to the Constitution, he did not have to answer any questions that might help to prove him guilty of a crime. However, by using this constitutional right, he turned the jurors sympathy away from him because it looked like he was hiding information.[5] Rosenberg continued to refuse to answer questions many times during his testimony.

The Greenglasses

Bloch then switched his questions to the Jell-O box. He asked if Rosenberg had ever been involved in any situation with a Jell-O-box. No, said Rosenberg. "Had he cut the side of a Jell-O box?" asked Bloch. No, Rosenberg said.

Rosenberg also said that he never talked about being a spy with Max Elitcher. He claimed never to have met Harry Gold and not to know Elizabeth Bentley. He said that his wife had never typed spy notes, and he denied that he had asked for or received any espionage information from the Greenglasses or anyone else.

Julius Rosenberg's description of other incidents differed from the testimony of the Greenglasses. For example, in 1945, just before Ruth Greenglass left New York City for New Mexico, Julius Rosenberg had visited her. Greenglass said that her husband was planning to take some items from the Army and would use them to make money. Rosenberg told her to, "warn David not to do anything foolish" because he will get "in trouble."[6] Rosenberg testified that after that incident, he had not heard anything more about Greenglass and Army trouble.

Bloch moved on to 1946. By this time, Rosenberg and the two Greenglass brothers, David and Bernie, had formed their own business. Over the next few years, David Greenglass often borrowed small amounts of money from the business that he never repaid. According to Julius

Rosenberg, David Greenglass seldom put in a full week of work. The business never had any dealings with the Soviet Union. In late 1949, David Greenglass left the business, demanding one thousand dollars for his share. Rosenberg told him he did not have that much money. Months passed, and in May 1950, David Greenglass asked to talk to Julius Rosenberg.

Greenglass demanded that Rosenberg give him two thousand dollars immediately. Rosenberg said he did not have any money. When he asked why this much money was needed, Greenglass refused to answer. Then Greenglass asked if Rosenberg would get a certificate for a smallpox shot from his doctor (supposedly so that he could travel out of the United States, away from his impending arrest). Rosenberg agreed to do this. But Rosenberg's doctor refused.

The next time Greenglass talked with Rosenberg, he again demanded money. When Rosenberg said no, Greenglass told him he would be sorry if he did not meet his demands. Rosenberg testified that he never gave Greenglass money. Throughout his testimony, Rosenberg insisted he was innocent of all charges.

Cross-examination

Then Irving Saypol cross-examined Julius Rosenberg. During his questioning, Saypol focused on Rosenberg's political views, not his views on the atomic bomb. First Saypol asked about Rosenberg's college friendships. Rosenberg hedged, then refused to answer. Saypol asked

Rosenberg about any groups to which he may have belonged while in college. Rosenberg tried to dodge these questions. Finally, he said that if Saypol was asking about the Communist party, he refused to answer.

Saypol later asked about a collection can. The FBI had seized it during its search of the Rosenbergs' apartment. The can was to be used to raise money for a Communist group. Rosenberg explained that a union, the International Workers Order, had sent him the can, but Rosenberg had not asked for it. Saypol was trying to show a link between this union and Communist activities.

Saypol's final set of questions centered on whether the Rosenbergs had gone to a certain photographer in May or June 1950. Rosenberg avoided direct answers. Then, he admitted that he may have gone to that photographer. But if he had, he would have asked for family photos, not passport photos.

Ethel Rosenberg

On the afternoon of March 26, the second defense witness, Ethel Rosenberg, was called to the witness stand. Alexander Bloch asked a series of questions about her education, marriage, and family. She said that in late 1944 and for most of the following year, she and her oldest son had been in poor health. This information was meant to show that she would have had little energy to be involved in a supposed spy ring.

When talking about the couple's furniture, Rosenberg said that most came from friends who had left it with the

Rosenbergs when they moved to California. She then spoke about the table that had been discussed in earlier testimonies. It had been delivered from Macy's either in 1944 or 1945 and had been paid for by her husband, said Rosenberg. He had bought it for twenty or twenty-one dollars.

Bloch asked where her typewriter had come from. Rosenberg explained that she had bought it from an actor when she was eighteen years old. She had used it to type Julius Rosenberg's college papers. After they were married, she typed some of his government work on it. When Bloch asked if she had typed anything that related to America's defense, Ethel Rosenberg said no.

Judge Kaufman then fired a question at the witness. Had she known of the government's charges against her husband in 1945? This was the time when Julius Rosenberg was fired from his job because the government had evidence of his Communist activities. Yes, she answered, supposedly he was a member of the Communist party. The judge asked if this was the reason for his dismissal from his job. For the first time, Ethel Rosenberg refused to answer a question. Like her husband, she then continued to refuse to answer many other questions during her testimony.

The Greenglasses

When asked if she had tried to convince Ruth Greenglass to ask David Greenglass to be a spy, Ethel Rosenberg said no. Bloch had other questions for her about this time in 1944. Had Julius Rosenberg dropped out of local Communist activities because he was doing other work for the Soviets?

No, she said. She also testified that her husband did not know David Greenglass was working on the atomic bomb. They had not found this out until 1946.

Had Ethel Rosenberg listened to her husband tell the Greenglasses, in late 1944 or early 1945, about the great power of the atomic bomb? Did she know he felt the information about this weapon should be shared with the Soviets? Ethel Rosenberg denied any conversation like this at any time. Then, the judge asked her for her political views on this matter. Rosenberg refused to answer.

Bloch turned his questions to the Jell-O box. Rosenberg said she had never heard anything about cutting a Jell-O box for spy work. She did say that she had boxes of Jell-O in the apartment.

Rosenberg denied typing atomic bomb information for her husband. She also denied copying any such information from her brother. Neither she nor her husband had given the Greenglasses money in 1944 or 1945. No spy notes were ever burned.

She told the jury that she loved David Greenglass, her youngest brother. Bloch asked if she knew Yakovlev, Bentley, Gold, or Dr. Fuchs. No, she said. When asked whether her husband was involved in any spying activity for the Russians, she said no. Ethel Rosenberg's description of David Greenglass's demand for two thousand dollars supported what Julius Rosenberg had said.

Ethel Rosenberg's testimony countered what the Greenglasses had said. She claimed that the Greenglasses were jealous of the Rosenbergs' relationship and upset over money lost in the failed, joint businesses.[7] Over and over again, Ethel Rosenberg insisted she was innocent of all charges.

Cross-examination

Ethel Rosenberg then faced a long cross-examination by Saypol. Part of his strategy was to show that Rosenberg's grand jury testimony in August 1950 differed from what she had just said. For most of her grand jury testimony, she had refused to answer questions. For example, during this trial, she had said various things about the Greenglasses. But before the grand jury, she had refused to answer many of these same questions. Saypol continually pointed out these inconsistencies as he read her own testimony to her.

Saypol asked her to explain herself. At first, Ethel Rosenberg could not answer. Judge Kaufman told her to come up with a reason. Finally, she said that at the time of the grand jury hearing, both her husband and brother were under arrest. She had heard that her brother might be trying to show that she, too, was involved in spying activities.

At the time of the Rosenbergs' trial, what Saypol was doing was legal. He could show that grand jury testimony and court trial testimony were not the same. However, in 1957, the United States Supreme Court ruled that this type of questioning was illegal. This rule was still six years away, though.

So Saypol continued to hammer at Rosenberg with more questions. She kept replying that she could not remember why she had refused to answer the same questions back then. Her answers made the jury question her credibility.[8]

She told the jury, "I didn't believe I was guilty then [at the time of the grand jury], I don't believe it today."[9]

Two More Witnesses

The defense called two other witnesses to testify. One, John Gibbons, was asked to identify a photo of Harry Gold that had run in the *New York Herald Tribune*. Gibbons was an employee of the *Tribune*.

The other witness, Thomas C. Kelley, worked at Macy's. When asked to produce records that showed that the Rosenbergs had bought a table at Macy's, Kelley could not comply. His company only kept records for four years. If the Rosenbergs were telling the truth, no paperwork existed to show this.

Summaries

After the defense had finished presenting its witnesses, both sides gave closing statements. During these speeches, both sides made final summaries of the facts and tried to discredit the other side's witnesses and evidence. Since the federal government presented its evidence first, it gave its summary last.

Manny Bloch spoke for the Rosenbergs on March 28, 1951. The packed courtroom listened quietly to his summary. He pointed out that the evidence in this case was all word-of-mouth. There was no physical evidence admitted during the trial that connected the Rosenbergs with any

David and Ruth Greenglass claimed the Russians had given the Rosenbergs a table outfitted for microfilming stolen documents. The Rosenbergs denied this charge. The table could not be located for the trial. This is a copy of a similar table, and was used as evidence during the trial.

crime. The government had not submitted the Jell-O box pieces, original sketches, notes, or any other physical evidence that linked the Rosenbergs directly with their alleged crimes.

Saypol summed up for the government. He reminded the jury of the evidence presented against the Rosenbergs by the Greenglasses and Harry Gold. He then said, "These conspirators stole the most important secrets ever known to mankind and delivered them to the Soviet Union. No defendants ever stood before the bar of American justice less deserving of sympathy."[10]

The Rosenberg-Sobell trial had run for fourteen days. The jury had listened to dozens of witnesses present a great deal of testimony. Then it was up to eleven men and one woman to decide whether it was the government's witnesses or the Rosenbergs who were telling the truth.

chapter six

THE DECISION

THE COURTHOUSE—On March 28, 1951, Judge Kaufman began instructing the jury. Before the jury members left to deliberate, he told them that they were responsible for arriving at a verdict of guilty or not guilty for Julius Rosenberg, Ethel Rosenberg, and Morton Sobell. To do this, the jury members were to evaluate the evidence and determine if the federal government had shown that the defendants were guilty beyond a reasonable doubt.

To be sure the jury would remember important terms used during the trial, Judge Kaufman covered definitions such as reasonable doubt, evidence, espionage, and conspiracy. He then discussed the espionage law that was at the heart of the case. Although the Soviet Union was a friend and ally during the time of the alleged spying activities, it was still not right to transfer secret information as a spy.

Judge Kaufman briefly reviewed some of the critical testimony and evidence presented in the case. Whether or not the defendants were Communists, he said, had no bearing on the verdict. He also pointed out that the testimony presented by the government's witnesses was quite different from the defendants' testimony. It was up to the jury members to judge the facts and make their own decision.

As he had throughout the trial, Judge Kaufman reminded the jury that a defendant's refusal to answer questions should not affect the verdict. Finally he said that he would determine the punishment, not the jury.

The Jury Deliberates

Once Judge Kaufman finished his instructions, a United States marshal led the handcuffed defendants and their lawyers to a room in the basement of the federal courthouse. Immediately after that, another federal marshal took the jury members into a large room almost directly above where the defendants waited.

The jury was to take whatever time it needed to go over the case and reach a verdict for each defendant. Inside the jury room were a long table, chairs, paper, and pencils. After all the jurors filed in, the door was locked. No one other than the jurors was permitted to hear what was discussed in the jury room.

Deliberating As a Juror

There is no set procedure that jurors must follow when deliberating a case. Each jury decides how to hold discussions, settle differences of opinion, and vote. Many judges tell the jurors the following when they deliberate:

- Jurors must discuss the evidence presented on all important issues before taking a vote on the verdict.

- Each juror should express his or her opinion during the deliberations.

- No juror should be pressured into changing a vote in order to arrive at a verdict more quickly.

- Each juror should weigh opposing views carefully.

- Any juror can change his or her vote if a discussion has changed a point of view.

The jurors began to deliberate right after a dinner break. At about 6:30 P.M., the jury asked for a copy of the indictment and a list of all witnesses. The information was sent to the jury, and the waiting continued.

At 8:10 P.M., the judge and lawyers were told that the jury was asking for some of Ruth Greenglass's testimony. Manny Block asked if the jury would also read the cross-examination of Greenglass. The judge reminded Bloch that the jury would get only what it requested. If the jury members decided they needed other testimony, then they would ask for it. The jury never asked for it.

At 9:45 P.M., the defendants and their lawyers were told that the jury members asked to see all of the evidence in the case. This was given to them. At 12:10 A.M., the judge told the jury to continue its deliberations. But the jury asked that it be allowed to end its present session. Although it had reached a verdict on two of the three defendants, it wanted to continue in the morning. The judge agreed. The jury would meet again at 10 A.M., March 29, 1951.

The Verdict

After a total of eight hours and forty-five minutes of deliberation, the jury announced that it had reached its verdicts. The judge ordered the defendants and their lawyers to come to the courtroom. Once they were seated, the jury filed into the courtroom and sat in the jury box.

Judge Kaufman ordered the defendants to rise. The Rosenbergs and Morton Sobell stood. Vincent Lebonite, the foreperson, or leader of the jury, was asked if the jury had reached a verdict. Yes, said Lebonite.

He then announced, "We find the defendant Julius Rosenberg guilty as charged. We find the defendant Ethel Rosenberg guilty as charged. We find the defendant Morton Sobell guilty as charged."[1] All three had been found guilty of conspiracy to commit espionage. Judge Kaufman could sentence them to death or jail them for up to thirty years.

Bloch was shaking as he asked the judge if he could poll the jury. This traditional court procedure is done to see if a juror might change his or her mind at the last minute. Each juror confirmed the verdict of guilty for each defendant.

Judge Kaufman expressed his appreciation for the jury's hard work. He also told them he agreed with their verdict. "My own opinion is that your verdict is a correct verdict."[2] He described the crime committed by the defendants as "loathsome."[3] The judge's comment about the verdict was an example of inappropriate behavior during the trial.

Irving Saypol, the prosecuting attorney, asked to speak. His speech echoed what the judge had said. Then Manny Bloch made an unusual speech. First he thanked the court and jury. He then said, "I feel satisfied by reason of the length of time that you [the jury] took for your deliberations, as well as the questions asked during the course of your deliberations."[4]

The jury foreperson later reported that nearly all the jurors had agreed immediately that all the defendants were guilty. Only one juror, a man, held out against voting guilty for Ethel Rosenberg. He worried that she would receive a death sentence with a guilty verdict, and that her children would be left without a mother.[5] He finally changed his mind so that the jurors were unanimous in their verdicts.

Judge Kaufman told the defendants he would sentence them in one week on April 5. The defendants, now called convicts, put on their winter coats. Once outside, many reporters took their photos and shouted at them. Their steps from the building to the waiting cars were recorded on film. Federal marshals pulled the Rosenbergs apart and they were whisked back to prison.

The Sentencing

The Rosenberg-Sobell verdicts were widely covered in the American press. The media ran rumors about what would happen next. Some New York newspapers claimed that death sentences would be given to all three. This, in turn, would scare the defendants into naming other members of their spy ring. No one knew where these rumors came from.

The only person who would deliver the actual sentences was Judge Kaufman. Once the jury gave its verdicts, he alone was responsible for deciding the fates of the defendants. In fact, Judge Kaufman asked prosecuting lawyer Saypol not to give the federal government's recommendation on sentencing. Usually, the judge asks for and gets a recommendation from the prosecution. Judge Kaufman explained, "The responsibility is so great that I believe the Court alone should assume the responsibility."[6] He said that he alone would decide the sentences. But Kaufman was not being truthful. In yet another example of inappropriate behavior by the judge, he asked for and got opinions from many sources including other federal judges, the prosecuting lawyers, and the FBI. J. Edgar Hoover, head of the FBI, recommended that Ethel Rosenberg not be given the death sentence. Perhaps, he too, was worried that her children would be left with no one if both Ethel and Julius were killed.

On April 5, 1951, Ethel and Julius Rosenberg were driven to the federal courthouse. By the time they reached the courtroom, the place was jammed with reporters and spectators. Even the hallways were packed. "The public was eager to see the ultimate punishment [given] out to these despised Communists," reported one member of the press.[7]

The Rosenbergs, holding hands tightly, stood in front of Judge Kaufman. Just before announcing the Rosenbergs' sentences, a nearby church bell began to toll. It rang twelve times, announcing the noon hour.

Judge Kaufman raised his voice to be heard over the ringing bell. He said,

> Your crime is worse than murder. I believe your conduct in putting in the hands of the Russians the A-bomb [atomic bomb] years before our best scientists predicted Russia would perfect the bomb has already caused the Communist aggression in Korea.[8]

To Judge Kaufman, the Rosenbergs' spying activities had led to Russia's creation of the atomic bomb. This, in turn, led to Russia's increased political activities in other countries, which helped to start the Korean War. People in the courtroom cried out as Judge Kaufman finished.

He then announced their sentences. "The sentence of the Court upon Julius and Ethel Rosenberg is, for the crime for which you have been convicted, you are hereby sentenced to the punishment of death."[9] Their sentences, death in the electric chair, would be carried out during the week of May 21, 1951. Next, he sentenced Morton Sobell to thirty years in jail. The judge recommended that Sobell serve the full sentence. Reporters ran out of the courtroom to pass on news of the verdicts.

As the Rosenbergs turned to leave, four United States marshals stood alongside them. They walked the couple to the basement, where they were locked into separate cells. Soon Ethel Rosenberg began to sing. Julius Rosenberg could hear his wife and shouted encouragement. She sang for more than an hour. Later that evening, the two were returned to their regular, but separate, jail cells.

The next day, April 6, Judge Kaufman sentenced David

Greenglass to fifteen years in prison. The judge said he recognized Greenglass's help in bringing to justice the others involved, specifically Julius and Ethel Rosenberg. He praised Greenglass for his courage to testify and for his help in stopping further espionage activities.

The Prisoners

Ethel Rosenberg was jailed in the women's house of detention in New York. Julius Rosenberg remained in a New York City prison. Sobell and Greenglass also were jailed in the same prison, but the three men were kept separate from each other.

On the morning of April 11, Ethel Rosenberg was moved out of her prison cell. Without any notice to her or to her lawyer, she was taken to Sing-Sing Prison in Ossining, New York. This is where she would be put to death in the electric chair. She was housed there as the only female prisoner in the Condemned Cells.

For a month, Ethel Rosenberg was jailed in nearly complete isolation. The Rosenbergs communicated only through their lawyer or by letters. A month later, Julius was also moved to Sing-Sing. Soon after his move, the Rosenbergs were allowed to meet in the prison's conference room along with their lawyer. As soon as they saw each other, the couple hugged and kissed, but guards quickly pulled them apart. It was the last time the Rosenbergs were able to hug each other.

The two were placed in separate cells, about thirty feet apart. A concrete hallway, heavy metal doors, and iron bars kept them apart. Yet at times Julius Rosenberg heard his wife sing for him. Hearing Ethel sing always cheered Julius Rosenberg.[10] Sometimes he would sing back.

The two were allowed to meet briefly on Wednesday mornings. At these times, Julius Rosenberg would sit in a steel cage close to Ethel's cell. Once a month, their lawyer visited them. A few times, their children came for short visits. Julius and Ethel Rosenberg continued to write loving, supportive letters to each other throughout their long appeals process.

chapter seven

WHERE DO WE STAND TODAY?

BATTLE CONTINUES— Lawyers for Julius and Ethel Rosenberg continued their legal fight. For more than two years, they filed various appeals. An appeal is a legal request to review a case that has already gone through the trial process and ended with a guilty verdict.

Appeals

The Rosenbergs' case had not closed completely. Manny Bloch filed his first major appeal on November 5, 1951, with the United States Court of Appeals, Second Circuit. The long appeal listed various reasons why this three-judge panel should overturn (reverse) Judge Irving Kaufman's sentences. One reason was that the government had not established definite guilt of the Rosenbergs. Another was that Judge Kaufman had not given the Rosenbergs a fair trial. Finally, Bloch stated that the sentences were "cruel and unusual punishment," which violated the Eighth Amendment.[1]

On January 10, 1952,

almost nine months after the sentencing, three judges listened to Bloch's appeal. For six weeks, the Rosenbergs and Bloch waited for the court's ruling. On February 25 the court said that it had carefully examined the trial record to see if it contained any of the errors listed in Bloch's appeal. All the judges agreed that the death sentence for the Rosenbergs was not unconstitutional and would stand.

Judge Jerome Frank suggested that Bloch appeal to the United States Supreme Court, the highest in the United States. Perhaps the Supreme Court would change the death sentences.

Following the judge's suggestion, Bloch filed an appeal with the Supreme Court of the United States. This court could only review the Appeals Court's findings, to see if any legal errors had been made in the decision. It could not review the trial to determine if the Rosenbergs had gotten a fair trial. On October 13, 1952, Bloch reported the bad news to the Rosenbergs—the Supreme Court had decided not to review the Appeals Court's findings.

Bloch did not give up. He immediately filed a request with the Supreme Court for a rehearing to reconsider their decision. On November 17, 1952, the Court declined the request. On December 21, 1952, nearly one thousand supporters stood outside Sing-Sing Prison and sang holiday songs to show support for the Rosenbergs. The next day, the couple received the news from Judge Kaufman. He had set January 12, 1953, as the date for their executions. By this time, the world had taken up the Rosenbergs' cause.

A Great Outcry

Throughout the arrest and trial of the Rosenbergs, the Communist party in America remained silent about the case. The silence was probably due to the hunt for Communists still going on in the United States. By the early 1950s, the number of members in the Communist party had sharply declined. At the time of the Rosenbergs' trial, all the top Communist leaders had been convicted of conspiring to teach and advocate the overthrow of the American government.

After the Rosenbergs' death sentences were announced, the Communist party protested. On April 6, 1951, the *Daily Worker*, the party's official newspaper, published an editorial on the Rosenbergs. The headline read, "Rosenbergs Sentenced to Death: Made Scapegoats for Korean War."[2] The editorial, in summary, said that their sentences were extreme and inhumane.

A national weekly magazine, the *National Guardian*, soon joined the cause. On August 15, 1951, the editors published an article that said the Rosenbergs were innocent. From August 22 to October 3, 1951, the editors ran a series of seven articles about the Rosenbergs' case. The articles "condemned the Rosenberg trial and conviction as one gigantic frame-up" by the FBI.[3] The Rosenbergs, said the articles, were victims of anticommunist hysteria fanned by the federal government. As the *National Guardian* continued its coverage of the case, Ethel Rosenberg sent support letters from prison to the magazine. All were published.

On October 10, 1951, the *National Guardian* told its readers that a committee to help the Rosenbergs had been formed. This was the National Committee to Secure Justice in the Rosenberg Case (NCSJRC), located in New York City. The organization's goals were to publicize the facts of the case and to raise money for court appeals for the Rosenbergs. Similar committees were formed in Great Britain, France, and Italy. By the end of 1952, the major countries of Western and Eastern Europe as well as Israel had established their own committees.

Throughout the rest of 1951, the American Communist party remained quiet about the Rosenbergs' case. Then on February 28, 1952, the party's newspaper, the *Daily Worker*, told its readers, "The Rosenberg case is a ghastly [horrible] political frame-up."[4] Two weeks later, another communist organization, the Civil Rights Congress, released a statement to the press, asking for people across America to support the Rosenbergs.

These organizations and publications, along with increased Communist activity, helped promote the Rosenbergs' cause. During 1952 and 1953, activities throughout the United States in support of the Rosenbergs included rallies, parades, picketing of public offices, prayer meetings, vigils, and delegations to Congress and other public offices. Members of the Communist party distributed hundreds of thousands of pamphlets and letters throughout the country. They circulated petitions that were signed by thousands, asking that the Rosenbergs' lives be spared. Supporters of the Rosenbergs sent thousands of letters and telegrams to public officials, including the president of the United States.

Soon after the Rosenbergs' cause was launched in America, people throughout the world joined in the effort to save them. American embassies in Canada and Europe received many petitions by various organizations and individuals. Demonstrations were held in major capital cities of Europe including Paris, France; Rome, Italty; and London, England. Newspapers in Ireland, Germany, Poland, Italy, and Austria ran front-page articles about the Rosenbergs.

Communists throughout Europe and the United States defended the Rosenbergs, saying they were innocent.

Appeal to the President

On December 30, 1952, Manny Bloch asked Judge Kaufman to reduce the sentence for the Rosenbergs. On January 6, 1953, Judge Kaufman granted a stay (hold) of execution for the Rosenbergs, but on one condition: Bloch had to file a petition for clemency (leniency) with the president of the United States, asking that the Rosenbergs' lives be spared.

The newly elected president, Dwight D. Eisenhower, denied the petition on February 11. He wrote,

> These two individuals have been tried and convicted for a most serious crime against the American people. . . . By their act these two individuals have, in fact, betrayed the cause of freedom for which free men are fighting and dying at this very hour. [The president was referring to the Korean War.]

He continued,

I have made a careful examination into this case, and I am satisfied that the two individuals have been accorded [given] their full measure of justice. I have determined that it is my duty in the interest of the people of the United States, not to set aside the verdict.[5]

Bloch filed more appeals with the Circuit Court of Appeals, Second Circuit, and again with the United States Supreme Court. The sentences remained, and, finally, Judge Kaufman set the execution date for June 18, 1953.

New Twist

Only days before the Rosenbergs' execution, two new lawyers, Fyke Farmer and Daniel Marshall, tried to help. Both lawyers had been hired by Irwin Edelman, a supporter of the Rosenbergs.

The two lawyers had developed a daring plan. On June 16, 1953, they went to see Supreme Court Associate Justice William O. Douglas. Justice Douglas was in his office, packing books. He was getting ready to go on summer vacation. Farmer and Marshall told Justice Douglas that Judge Kaufman had not followed the law correctly. The Rosenbergs had been tried and convicted under the Espionage Act of 1917 and sentenced to death by the judge. But, in 1946, Congress had passed the Atomic Energy Act. This law said that only a jury could recommend the death sentence, not a judge.

Justice Douglas listened to the two lawyers. He asked them to put together the Rosenbergs' trial records and a statement of their legal points. Working with Bloch, the lawyers pulled together the requested information in an hour. Farmer and Marshall sped back to the Supreme Court. Justice Douglas took the information from them, then said he planned to work all night, if needed, to go through everything.

Meanwhile, Bloch flew from Washington, D. C., to New York City, bringing another request for clemency with him to Sing-Sing prison. Both Julius and Ethel Rosenberg needed to sign this request. Bloch also brought their sons, Michael and Robert, to the prison. If everything failed, this would be the last time the Rosenberg family would be together. After getting the signatures, Bloch then brought the clemency request and the children to Washington, D.C.

On June 17, 1953, Justice Douglas announced that the executions were on hold. He also sent the case back to the district court in New York to determine if the Atomic Energy Act of 1946 should have beeen used to determine sentences. Whatever the outcome, the case would return to the Supreme Court. Since the Supreme Court was not in session until early October, the Rosenbergs had a few more months to live. Reporters quickly spread the news as Bloch, Farmer, and Marshall celebrated.

Final Days

Their joy was short-lived, however. Herbert Brownell, the United States attorney general, did not agree with the Supreme Court's decision. To rule on Brownell's challenge, Chief Justice Fred Vinson called the entire Supreme Court back in session on June 18. Justice Douglas was already on his summer vacation, but he came back to Washington, D.C. Justice Hugo Black left his hospital bed to return to the Supreme Court. He had been scheduled for surgery.[6]

The Rosenbergs' lawyers presented their case to the Supreme Court. The next morning, on June 19, the Supreme Court decided that the Rosenbergs had been tried and sentenced correctly under the Espionage Act of 1917. The Atomic Energy Act of 1946 did not apply to the Rosenbergs' trial. (The crimes had been committed in 1944 and 1945. Therefore, a 1946 law could not be applied. To do so would have been unconstitutional.) The vote was six to three. Judge Kaufman's death sentence stood, and the executions would occur at 8:00 P.M., that same night. American and international reporters rushed outside the Supreme Court building to spread the news.

Thousands gathered near Union Square in New York City. Across America, thousands of people sent mail and telegrams to the president, asking that he spare the Rosenbergs' lives. Huge crowds rallied for the Rosenbergs in Canada, Israel, Mexico, South America, parts of Africa, and in major Eastern and Western European cities.

None of this swayed President Eisenhower. That evening, he denied the Rosenbergs' final request for clemency, saying, "I will not intervene in this matter."[7]

On their final day, Julius and Ethel Rosenberg were allowed to sit in the same room and talk. A wire mesh screen kept them apart. Just before Julius Rosenberg was taken to the electric chair, he put two fingers to his lips and pressed his fingers on the screen. Ethel Rosenberg did the same

President Dwight D. Eisenhower refused to grant Julius and Ethel Rosenberg clemency.

thing. As they touched through the screen, they pressed so hard that blood ran from their fingers. At 8:03 P.M., Julius Rosenberg died in the electric chair. Ethel Rosenberg died at 8:17 P.M. Thousands of people attended their funeral in Brooklyn, New York.

Continuing Controversy

Immediately after Julius and Ethel Rosenberg were executed, the Communist party ran a four-page article in the *Daily Worker*. The article spoke out against the Rosenbergs' unjust trial and execution by the federal government. Other newspaper editorials, though, said that the Rosenbergs had had a fair trial. An editorial in the *Philadelphia Tribune*, published on June 23, 1953, summed up what many felt, "Americans who betray their country by assisting the enemy must expect the consequences of their acts."[8]

Yet others questioned whether the death sentences were too severe for their crimes. Other convicted spies had spent time in jail; none were executed for their crimes. Harry Gold, for example, got thirty years in jail. David Greenglass received fifteen years. Some people were morally against execution, especially because Ethel Rosenberg was the mother of two young children.

In 1975, the sons of Julius and Ethel Rosenberg published a book, *We Are Your Sons*. After their parents' death, both were adopted by Anne and Abel Meeropol. In their book, Robert and Michael Meeropol state that their parents were innocent. They present an assortment of information to support their claim. Their book contains many of the letters their parents wrote from prison. In their final letter to their children, Julius and Ethel Rosenberg wrote, "Always remember that we were innocent and could not wrong our conscience."[9]

Also in the same year, another book that re-examined the case came out. This book, *The Unquiet Death of Julius and Ethel Rosenberg*, was funded by the Corporation for Public Broadcasting, a government-supported organization. The book was based on a television documentary of the same name. The documentary and book raised many questions about the Rosenbergs' trial and execution.

Since then, various books and articles about the Rosenberg case have been published. Some say the Rosenbergs should not have been executed. The author of the 1989 book *Fatal Error* concluded that the Rosenbergs' execution was illegal. They had been tried under the wrong law.

During the 1990s, the federal government released newly declassified information about World War II and the Rosenberg case. In 1995 the National Security Agency released the Venona Cables, decoded World War II Soviet spy documents, that show that the Rosenbergs had been Soviet spies. Decoded Soviet messages released by the United States National Security Council in 1995 indicate that Julius Rosenberg, did, in fact, run a spy ring. Ethel Rosenberg was not implicated in these documents.

Some Soviet sources have said that the Rosenbergs were spies. Papers written by Nikita Khrushchev, head of the Soviet Union from 1957 to 1964, mentioned that Julius

Rosenberg spied for the Soviets. Khruschev's papers were published in a 1990 book. Other evidence came from former Soviet secret police in the late 1990s who stated that the Rosenbergs had been spies.

In a 1983 book that was reprinted in 1997 with a new introduction, the authors of *The Rosenberg File* examined the case in light of all this latest information. When they first started researching their book, both authors maintained that the Rosenbergs were innocent. However, after years of research, they concluded that Julius Rosenberg had headed a spy ring. Ethel Rosenberg had only minor involvement.

Many plays, poems, songs, movies, videos, art works, magazine articles, and books have been created about Julius and Ethel Rosenberg. Each one continues the controversy: Were they guilty of conspiracy to commit espionage? Or were they victims of their political beliefs, unable to get a fair trial due to the strong anticommunist atmosphere at that time? They were executed—did the punishment fit the crime? If the Rosenbergs were spies, why did they never tell the government the names of other spies? Finally, why did the Rosenbergs always say they were innocent? These are questions that can only be answered by speculation today. People must form their own opinions, based on their interpretations of the facts. What do you think?

Questions for Discussion

1. Why do you think the Rosenberg case has remained famous for so long?

2. Do you think the police had probable cause to arrest Julius Rosenberg and Ethel Rosenberg? Why or why not?

3. Defendants do not have to testify during their trial. Was it a good idea that the Rosenbergs testified? Why or why not?

4. The Rosenberg trial took place during the McCarthy era of distrust of Communists. How much influence, if any, did this have on the Rosenbergs' trial? Explain your answer.

5. Based on the information presented in this book, do you think the Rosenbergs were guilty or innocent of the charges against them? Explain your answer.

6. Compared to newspapers, what advantages did radio and television offer to those who followed the Rosenberg case?

7. Why did so many people protest what happened to the Rosenbergs?

8. Compare the sentence received by David Greenglass with those for Julius and Ethel Rosenberg. Were all of the sentences fair? Explain your answer.

9. If the Rosenberg trial were held today, would they have received a different sentence? Explain your answer.

Chapter Notes

Chapter 1. Arrested as Spies

There are no notes.

Chapter 2. America in the Early 1950s

1. Marc McCutcheon, *The Writer's Guide Everyday Life from Prohibition Through World War II* (Cincinnati, Ohio: Writer's Digest Books, 1995), p. 78.

2. Alvin H. Goldstein, *The Unquiet Death of Julius and Ethel Rosenberg* (New York: Lawrence Hill and Company, 1975), p. 20.

3. Russell Aiuto, "The Rosenbergs: A Case of Love, Espionage, Deceit, and Betrayal," © 1998, <http://www.crimelibrary.com/rosen/rosenmain.htm> (December 15, 2000).

4. Ilene Philipson, *Ethel Rosenberg: Beyond the Myths* (New Brunswick, N.J.: Rutgers University Press, 1988), p. 49.

5. Goldstein, p. 8.

6. Philipson, p. 95.

7. Ibid., 92.

8. Federal Bureau of Investigation, Freedom of Information Act, "Rosenberg Case Summary," September 25, 1953, <http://foia.fbi.gov/roberg.htm> (December 15, 2000).

9. Robert Meeropol and Michael Meeropol, *We Are Your Sons: The Legacy of Ethel and Julius Rosenberg* (Boston: Houghton Mifflin Company, 1975), p. 85.

10. Ibid., p. 88.

Chapter 3. The Road to Court

1. Federal Bureau of Investigation, Freedom of Information Act, "Rosenberg Case Summary," September 25, 1953, <http://foia.fbi.gov/roberg.htm> (December 15, 2000).

2. Ibid.

3. Ilene Philipson, *Ethel Rosenberg: Beyond the Myths* (New Brunswick, N.J.: Rutgers University Press, 1988), p. 235.

4. Ronald Radosh and Joyce Milton, *The Rosenberg File* (New Haven, Conn.: Yale University Press, 1997), p. 87.

5. Philipson, pp. 249–250.

6. Federal Bureau of Investigation, "Rosenberg Case Summary."

7. Philipson, p. 275.

Chapter 4. The Case for the Federal Government

1. Federal Bureau of Investigation, Freedom of Information Act, "Rosenberg Case Summary," September 25, 1953, <http://foia.fbi.gov/roberg.htm> (December 15, 2000).

2. Louis Nizer, *The Implosion Conspiracy* (New York: Doubleday and Company, Inc., 1973), p. 48.

3. Federal Bureau of Investigation, "Rosenberg Case Summary."

4. Ibid.

5. Ibid.

6. Ibid.

7. Ibid.

8. Ibid.

9. Ibid.

10. Alvin H. Goldstein, *The Unquiet Death of Julius and Ethel Rosenberg* (New York: Lawrence Hill and Company, 1975), p. 30.

11. Russell Aiuto, "The Rosenbergs: A Case of Love, Espionage, Deceit, and Betrayal," 1998, The Crime Library, <http://www.crimelibrary.com/rosen/rosenmain.htm> (December 15, 2000).

12. Ibid.

13. Federal Bureau of Investigation, "Rosenberg Case Summary."

14. Nizer, p. 121.

15. Ilene Philipson, *Ethel Rosenberg: Beyond the Myths* (New Brunswick, N.J.: Rutgers University Press, 1988), p. 282.

16. Federal Bureau of Investigation, "Rosenberg Case Summary."

17. Ibid.

18. Russell Aiuto, "The Rosenbergs: A Case of Love, Espionage, Deceit, and Betrayal."

19. Federal Bureau of Investigation, "Rosenberg Case Summary."

Chapter 5. The Case for Julius and Ethel Rosenberg

1. Louis Nizer, *The Implosion Conspiracy* (New York: Doubleday and Company, Inc., 1973), p. 54.

2. Ibid., p. 55.

3. Ronald Radosh and Joyce Milton, *The Rosenberg File* (New Haven, Conn.: Yale University Press, 1997), p. 239.

4. Russell Aiuto, "The Rosenbergs: A Case of Love, Espionage, Deceit, and Betrayal," 1998, The Crime Library, <http://www.crimelibrary.com/rosen/rosenmain.htm> (December 15, 2000).

5. Ibid.

6. Radosh and Milton, p. 241.

7. Alvin H. Goldstein, *The Unquiet Death of Julius and Ethel Rosenberg* (New York: Lawrence Hill and Company, 1975), p. 36.

8. S. Andhil Fineberg, *The Rosenberg Case: Fact and Fiction* (New York: Oceana Publications, 1953), p. 30.

9. Radosh and Milton, p. 263.

10. Goldstein, p. 37.

Chapter 6. The Decision

1. Alvin H. Goldstein, *The Unquiet Death of Julius and Ethel Rosenberg* (New York: Lawrence Hill and Company, 1975), p. 39.

2. Louis Nizer, *The Implosion Conspiracy* (New York: Doubleday and Company, Inc., 1973), p. 340.

3. Ibid.

4. Federal Bureau of Investigation, Freedom of Information Act, "Rosenberg Case Summary," September 25, 1953, <http://foia.fbi.gov/roberg.htm> (December 15, 2000).

5. Goldstein, p. 41.

6. Ronald Radosh and Joyce Milton, *The Rosenberg File* (New Haven, Conn.: Yale University Press, 1997), p. 276.

7. Ilene Philipson, *Ethel Rosenberg: Beyond the Myths* (New Brunswick, N.J.: Rutgers University Press, 1988), p. 303.

8. Federal Bureau of Investigation, "Rosenberg Case Summary."

9. Ibid.

10. Russell Aiuto, "The Rosenbergs: A Case of Love, Espionage, Deceit, and Betrayal," 1998, The Crime Library, <http://www.crimelibrary.com/rosen/rosenmain.htm> (December 15, 2000).

Chapter 7. Where Do We Stand Today?

1. Federal Bureau of Investigation, Freedom of

Information Act, "Rosenberg Case Summary," September 25, 1953, <http://foia.fbi.gov/roberg.htm> (December 15, 2000).

2. Ibid.

3. Ibid.

4. Ibid.

5. Ibid.

6. Ibid.

7. Alvin H. Goldstein, *The Unquiet Death of Julius and Ethel Rosenberg* (New York: Lawrence Hill and Company, 1975), p. 39.

8. S. Andhil Fineberg, *The Rosenberg Case: Fact and Fiction* (New York: Oceana Publications, 1953), p. 148.

9. Robert and Michael Meeropol, *We Are Your Sons: The Legacy of Ethel and Julius Rosenberg* (Boston: Houghton Mifflin Company, 1975), p. 216.

Glossary

alibi—A defendant's reason why he or she could not have done what is alleged.

amendment—New provisions to, or changes to portions of the Constitution.

appeal—Asking a court with a higher authority to review the decision of a lower court.

atomic bomb—An extremely powerful nuclear weapon.

Bill of Rights—The first ten amendments to the United States Constitution. The Bill of Rights gives Americans many freedoms and protections such as freedom of religion, speech, and the press.

burden of proof—The amount of evidence required in a case in order for a jury to find in favor of the person bringing the lawsuit. The more serious the consequences of the case, the greater the amount of proof required.

closing arguments—At the end of the testimony, the lawyers for both sides sum up why they believe the jury should rule in their favor.

Cold War—The struggle between the democratic United States and its allies and the Communist Soviet Union and its allies that lasted from 1944 to 1991. Direct military conflict did not occur between these two countries. Instead, intense economic and diplomatic struggles erupted continually.

communism—A political system under which people support the common ownership and sharing of labor and products.

conspiracy—A secret plan to commit a crime.

counterintelligence—The activity of a department to block an enemy's information sources, to deceive the enemy, and to gather political and military information.

cross-examination—Questioning of a witness by the opposing lawyer.

cryptologists—People who study, figure out, and use secret codes.

defendant—A person on trial who is accused of a crime.

defense lawyer—A lawyer who acts on behalf of the person being accused in a trial.

deliberations—A jury's discussion and evaluation of the evidence presented in a trial.

espionage—The act of spying.

evidence—Any statement or object presented in a court case as a proof of fact.

expert witness—A person who has specialized knowledge or experience in some area who gets paid to testify at a trial as a recognized authority.

foreperson—Head of a jury; the person who leads or organizes the discussion of a jury and is responsible for trying to keep order.

grand jury—A jury that investigates criminal complaints and decides if someone should be formally charged with a committing a crime.

Great Depression—On October 29, 1929, stock values dropped drastically, and the New York Stock Exchange, the largest in the world, crashed. This led to the economic slump called The Great Depression.

immigrant—A person who comes to live permanently in a new country.

indictment—A formal written accusation prepared for a court by a grand jury. It outlines which crime or crimes are believed to have been committed and names the person or persons who probably committed those crimes.

jury—A group of people who have sworn to decide the facts in a court case and to reach a fair verdict or decision.

linguists—People who study languages.

mistrial—A trial that has no legal effect because of some error or serious misconduct during the trial.

opening statements—The presentation made by the lawyers on both sides of the case at the start of a trial. During opening statements, the issues and facts that will be presented are outlined. The purpose of the opening statements is to give the jury an overview of the case and to help them understand the evidence they will hear.

prosecutor—A government official authorized to accuse and prosecute (bring to trial) someone who is believed to have committed a crime. Prosecutors are known by various names in different parts of the United States: district attorney, state's attorney, and people's attorney.

sentence—In criminal cases, the decision by a jury or judge about what punishment is appropriate for a convicted defendant.

socialism—A doctrine or movement calling for public ownership of factories and other means of production.

testimony—Evidence given after taking an oath in court to tell the truth; questions answered under oath concerning what one knows about a case being heard in court.

United States Constitution—The highest law of America. This document, which went into effect in 1787, covers the basic laws and principles under which America is governed.

verdict—The decision that a jury or judge makes after hearing and considering all of the evidence and testimony in a case.

witness—Someone who has seen or heard something relating to a court case; someone who provides evidence about a case in a court.

Further Reading

Larsen, Anita. *The Rosenbergs.* New York: Crestwood House, Macmillan Publishing Co., 1992.

Meeropol, Michael, ed. *The Rosenberg Letters: A Complete Edition of the Prison Correspondence of Julius and Ethel Rosenberg.* New York: Garland Publishing, Inc., 1994.

Neville, John F. *The Press, the Rosenbergs and the Cold War.* Westport, Conn.: Greenwood Publishing Group, Inc., 1995.

Okun, Rob A., ed. *The Rosenbergs: Collected Visions of Artists and Writers.* New York: Universe Books, 1988.

Philipson, Irene. *Ethel Rosenberg: Beyond the Myths.* New Brunswick, N.J.: Rutgers University Press, 1988.

Radosh, Ronald and Joyce Milton. *The Rosenberg File.* New Haven, Conn.: Yale University Press, 1997.

Trager, Oliver C., ed. *Communism: The Final Crisis.* New York: Facts on File, 1990.

Internet Addresses

Russell Aiuto. "The Rosenbergs: A Case of Love, Espionage, Deceit, and Betrayal," © 1998, <http://www.crimelibrary.com/rosen/rosenmain.htm>.

Federal Bureau of Investigation. Freedom of Information Act, "Rosenberg Case Summary," September 25, 1953, <http://foia.fbi.gov/roberg.htm>.

Douglas Linder. University of Missouri at Kansas City, Famous Trials Web site, "Famous American Trials: Rosenbergs Trial 1951," © 1998, <http://www.law. umkc.edu/faculty/projects/ftrials/rosenb/ROSENB. HTM>.

———. Jurist Web site, Famous Trials, © 2000, "The Rosenberg Trial," <http://www.jurist.law.pitt.edu/ trials6.htm>.

Index